The Alpacas of Stormwind Farm

Ingrid Wood

authorHOUSE®

AuthorHouse™
1663 Liberty Drive
Bloomington, IN 47403
www.authorhouse.com
Phone: 1-800-839-8640

First published by AuthorHouse 8/25/2011

ISBN: 978-1-4634-2392-6 (sc)
ISBN: 978-1-4634-2393-3 (e)
ISBN: 978-1-4634-2394-0 (hc)

Library of Congress Control Number: 2011911259

Printed in the United States of America

ALSO BY INGRID WOOD

A Breeder's Guide to Genetics—Relax, it's not Rocket Science

For Benjamin, Rioghnan, and Grace

Contents

Illustrations

All images without a photo credit are courtesy of the author.

Front Cover: Claudia and Rupert (Courtesy Christina Piscitelli)

Back Cover: Ingrid and Tasman (Courtesy Julia Tysarzik)

Dust Jacket Flaps (Hardcover): Breeze's grandchildren (Courtesy Barbara Ewing)

Chapter 1:
The farm sign helps visitors find the entrance to our lane.

It's a farm!

Ingrid on Stormwind Farm (Courtesy Julia Tysarzik)

David and our nephew Jonas relax on the porch. (Courtesy Julia Tysarzik)

Chapter 2:
Breeze was sent to Serenity Alpacas to give birth to her first cria, Kalita. (Courtesy Harley D. Wood)

Harley as a handsome, young dude (Courtesy Hugh Masters)

Chapter 3:
Pearl and Riverman were never more than a few feet apart from each other.
(Courtesy Christina Piscitelli)

Riverman was adorable. (Courtesy Christina Piscitelli)

Riverman awaits Pearl's commands. (Courtesy Christina Piscitelli)

Chapter 4:
Two tough alpaca boys, Pilot and Hunter, prefer the outdoors to seeking shelter in their barn. (Courtesy Julia Tysarzik)

Cherry Ridge Tasman (Courtesy Barbara Ewing)

Halter Champion Bella Cria's Good Fortune (Courtesy Barbara Ewing)

Sure Shot's Traveling Man (Courtesy Barbara Ewing)

Chapter 5:
Dual Champion Stormwind's No No Josette, FCH was the first puppy born under the Stormwind prefix. (Courtesy Barbara Ewing)

Ingrid's friend, Kristin, plays with Chi-Chi in the fenced Whippet yard.

Chapter 6:
Eagle (Courtesy Harley D. Wood)

Triton consoled his friend Eagle when the latter was rejected by his dam. (Courtesy Barbara Ewing)

Chapter 7:
Ingrid administers a routine inoculation to Claudia. (Courtesy Julia Tysarzik)

Pearl supervises the daily dung removal from Stormwind Farm's pastures. (Courtesy Christina Piscitelli)

David mows the pasture with a diesel powered golf course mower. (Courtesy Julia Tysarzik)

Sure Shot's Traveling Man (T-Man) breeds Maribel. The leads were removed as soon as the photo was taken.

Chapter 8:
Spacious pastures help keep the peace among the alpacas on Stormwind Farm.

Maribel acts deferential toward her elders.

Chapter 9:
Sunflowers in full bloom attract bees and birds to Stormwind Farm. (Courtesy Julia Tysarzik)

Chapter 10:
Claudia and Rupert (Courtesy Christina Piscitelli)

The alpaca females check out Caramel's newborn cria.

Chapter 11:
A cria enjoys a sunny day in the fall.

Who can resist the charm of an alpaca cria? (Courtesy Barbara Ewing)

Two *Camelidynamics* workshop participants practice haltering techniques. (Courtesy Julia Tysarzik)

Chapter 12:
David shears a very pregnant Bella.

In 2010, we had the rare pleasure of having two helpers during two of our shearing days. John and Kristin Thorpe now offer shearing services to other alpaca owners.

Caramel

Carol Masters created these attractive and warm alpaca hats and scarves. (Courtesy Hugh Masters)

Chapter 13:

Black-eyed Susans and zinnias are Ingrid's favorite summer flowers.

Ingrid and Mariah walk on Stormwind Farm on a winter day. (Courtesy Harley D. Wood)

Chapter 14:
Ingrid and Dexter (Courtesy Julia Tysarzik)

Chapter 15:
Emily Stacy and her suri alpaca, Chiquita, wait to participate in a performance class. (Courtesy Sally Stacy)

The Stormwind Farm booth offers a variety of alpaca products to customers. (Courtesy Julia Tysarzik)

Foreword

As editor of *The International Camelid Quarterly* magazine, I have had the good fortune to read the works of many talented, and very knowledgeable, camelid breeders. Articles provided by Ingrid are always eagerly anticipated as they carry her personal perspective of an event or experience and are written in a clear, concise, and frank manner.

When Ingrid asked if I would write a foreword for this—her latest—book, I was both delighted and honored; delighted at the prospect of reading more of her work and honored to have been asked.

From beginning to end Ingrid maintains an easy, conversational tone, all the while imparting knowledge that she has acquired through her years of raising alpacas and Whippets. Although she clearly expresses the happiness and peace of mind a visit with her herd produces, at no time in her book does she lead us to believe raising alpacas is no more work than a skip through the pasture. While Ingrid is honest about the work involved in the raising of alpacas, she also writes vividly of the pleasure the animals have brought her. Reading about the arrival of the crias—and watching their personalities emerge—is as enjoyable as picturing the almost blissful expression on the faces of the freshly shorn alpacas as they receive a reprieve from the heat and humidity by way of a soaking from the garden hose.

I especially enjoyed *Chapter 11: Cria Songs*, perhaps because I am a mother who defied social acceptability and sang and cuddled my babies to sleep...it was soothing for all of us. You, as did I, may find the concept of singing to the crias initially surprising. However, as the chapter unfolds, the idea makes perfect sense. I'll not tell you anything more.

If you are new to the world of alpacas, or are seriously considering becoming a breeder, this is the perfect book—kept beside your bed or in your tote/briefcase—to read as free moments present themselves. It will be time well spent.

Sharon Parsons
Editor
The International Camelid Quarterly

Preface

"It's getting to be obvious even to skeptics that animals are smarter than we think."—Temple Grandin, *Animals in Translation.*

The first two importations of large groups of alpacas from Chile to the United States of America took place in 1983 and 1984. Since that time, numerous alpaca farms and ranches have been established in countries all over the world.

On the North American continent, the general public has become quite aware of the existence of alpacas and their end product, the buttery soft fiber that comes in so many colors.

People are not only curious about alpacas but are also eager to learn about farm life in general. Many have rather vague ideas of what it takes to raise and maintain livestock. Nevertheless, as consumers, they want to be assured that farm animals are treated humanely.

In *The Alpacas of Stormwind Farm,* I write about the joys as well as the challenges of farming with alpacas. The book's contents are not intended to cover all aspects of managing an alpaca farm; however, readers should find enough information to make an assessment what such a venture entails.

It is my hope that the book will also encourage readers to examine their premises about livestock and animals in general. Herd animals have rich social lives. In the case of domestic livestock such as alpacas, humans are included in the social circle. There are owners and breeders who believe that animals have no feelings and live by instinct alone. I do not agree with them. Some readers will no doubt feel that I anthropomorphize the alpacas living on Stormwind Farm.

I realize that alpacas are not people covered with fleeces. That does not mean that these sensitive animals do not feel contentment, fear, envy, grief, happiness, and a wide array of other emotions. Nobody who spends time with alpacas and observes them closely over a decade will ever view them merely as mindless producers of fiber, meat, and pelts. Much of the book's focus is therefore on the alpacas as distinct individuals within a larger herd structure.

Many authors write about their lives on a farm with style and elegance. Their books— while informative—read like poetry. Unfortunately, I am not one of those authors. I am well aware of my limitations as a writer and recognize that my work is not a literary masterpiece.

The Alpacas of Stormwind Farm is simply the story of my years living with the animals I call my pasture companions. Raising alpacas has blessed me with experiences and friendships that have been truly amazing and wonderful.

I hope the book gives my readers pleasure.

Acknowledgements

Thank you to my husband, David, who would happily live in a townhouse if given the opportunity but loyally supports my passion for farming and raising alpacas. He is my trusted handyman and alpaca shearer.

Thank you to Dave Belt. He edited the first draft of the manuscript.

Thank you to Caroline Johnson, a fellow alpaca breeder. She read the early manuscript and gave candid advice.

Thank you to Harley D. Wood (David), Barbara Ewing, Hugh Masters, Christina Piscitelli, and Julia Tysarzik for generously permitting me the use of their photographs.

Thank you to Kristin Thorpe, another alpaca breeder and a good friend. She helped organize and label my photos to get them ready for publication.

Thank you to Jovi Larson, Sharon Parsons, and Denise Como. They read the manuscript and permitted me to share their kind words of praise with my readers. Jovi is a long-time suri alpaca breeder, and Sharon is the editor of the *International Camelid Quarterly*. Denise is a friend, fellow sighthound owner, and the co-author of *A Breeder's Guide to Genetics – Relax, it's not Rocket Science*.

A special *thank you* to Carol Masters, my friend and mentor. She expertly typed the hand-written manuscript, corrected numerous drafts, helped prepare the manuscript for publication, and remained patient throughout the entire process. This book would never have been published without Carol's help.

The biggest *thank you* is reserved for the alpacas. They have enriched my life well beyond my expectations.

The farm sign helps visitors find the entrance to our lane.

Chapter 1

The Farm

The property we bought in 1995 and named Stormwind Farm was once part of a much larger land parcel. It measures not quite eight acres. As farms go, it is laughably small. People who are familiar with New Jersey real estate prices don't laugh. When they see Stormwind Farm, they're impressed with what my husband David and I have accomplished over the years.

"It's a play farm," David likes to joke. If that's true, we work pretty hard at playing.

In the early days, a few people questioned our definition of a farm.

"You raise livestock," a friend said, "shouldn't your place be called a ranch?"

"I thought a farm produces crops, not animals," was another comment.

Farm or ranch? When we first moved to the land, I didn't care about nomenclature. "Call it whatever you want," I replied to those who pondered the issue.

There were more important things to decide. We planned, for example, where to locate the barn and how much hay to buy so the supply would last until the next year's second cutting. Eventually, I became curious myself as to the proper definition of both words. It was time to consult the dictionary.

Our edition of *Webster's New World Dictionary* defines *farm* as *a piece of land (with house, barns, etc.) on which crops and animals are raised.* In the early years, we could point to a hayfield that had been planted and was annually harvested by a local farmer as evidence of a crop. As our alpaca herd grew, the hayfield was fenced in and became our largest and most productive pasture. Since we were no longer producing crops, did that mean that our land, technically speaking, was no longer a farm?

I looked up the word *ranch.* According to *Webster's,* it describes *a large farm, with its buildings, land, etc., for the raising of cattle, horses, or sheep in great numbers: term used especially in the western United States.* Descriptive words like large and great are all relative, of course. Quite possibly, a resident of New York City would consider our modest piece of land to be a large ranch. I decided that I would be embarrassed to look a Texas rancher in the eye after using that adjective/noun combination in connection with our eight acres.

Finally, there's the definition of a *farmstead: The land and buildings of a farm.* Where did that leave the alpacas? The word *farmette* popped into my mind. It's a tiny farm. To fit the category, the owner would also have to grow crops, in addition to livestock. It appeared that our land—where we raised alpacas on eight acres—did not fit neatly into any category. I closed the dictionary. Wait! There is the produce from my small vegetable garden, I thought. It'll have to cover the crop part of the farm definition. Stormwind Farm it was!

Occasionally, someone still asks, "Shouldn't your place be called a ranch?"

I think of the three hardy tomato plants and the spreading clumps of thyme, chives, oregano, and basil in my tiny garden. "No," I answer firmly, with my eyes twinkling, "we raise livestock as well as crops. It's a farm!"

People from other parts of the country are often surprised to hear that New Jersey has farmland. David and I are residents of Springfield

Township, a small community in Burlington County's farm belt. Our township covers roughly 19,000 acres, 8,000 of which are placed in New Jersey's popular Farm Preservation program. These protected acres can never be developed.

It's a farm!

Our own piece of land is not in the program but is zoned for farming. Due to zoning restrictions, it cannot be subdivided. The house we built is the only residence permitted on the property.

Springfield Township is divided into three "villages." We live on the outskirts of Jacksonville. Its tiny core consists of a convenience store, a firehouse, a very old and lovingly restored school serving as a community center, a privately run small zoo, and several private homes. At dusk, we hear the mournful cries of the zoo's peacocks.

The day after we had moved to the farm, a neighbor greeted me when I arrived home from work. "You missed the excitement," she reported, "a monkey escaped from the zoo down the road. It sunned itself on your layer of patio blocks."

The blocks were stacked near the kennel we had brought with us from our former suburban backyard. The small building is sided and shingled with locally grown Atlantic White Cedar. Over the years, the wood weathered to a beautiful, silvery grey. The building serves double duty as a garden shed. A section inside is portioned off to store my gardening tools.

Luckily, the attached kennel run had not been built yet on the day the monkey enjoyed its freedom. The dogs were safely locked in the house when the hairy visitor appeared on the farm. The Whippets, perched on the window sill in David's office, must have been in a frenzy while watching the monkey frolic in their yard.

The Whippet yard is quite spacious and allows the dogs to stretch their legs and run at full speed. It's securely fenced. The dogs can't leave, but—not surprisingly—the yard is not monkey-proof.

The shape of the entire farm is known around here as a flag lot. The road frontage is only two hundred feet. After the first two acres, the width of the property expands to four hundred feet. Visitors who drive up the long lane and reach the house can choose to park in one of two small graveled lots. House and parking areas are bordered by lawns and several beds planted with a mixture of bushes, perennials, and annual flowers. The lawn areas are purposely kept small. I had wanted as much pasture as possible.

The farm has four pastures. The original two pastures house our alpaca males. The larger two were added later and are reserved for females and crias. The pastures are enclosed with five-foot-high sturdy wire mesh fencing to keep out predators.

Once, when I longingly expressed the desire for more grazing space, my friend Helga poked fun at me. "You know how they say that you can never be too thin or too rich," she hooted, "except with you, it's that one can never have enough pastures or barns."

"You're right," David chimed in. Turning to Helga, he explained, only half kidding, "My wife is a land-hungry peasant."

How right he is! What he and many others will never understand is that my kind of land hunger is not about money. It's not about investments and profits. I quite literally would not exchange my small farm for a New York City penthouse worth millions of dollars.

"What is it then?" a friend once asked me.

I didn't try to explain. Those who share my hunger do not need an explanation. For those who do not, no amount of explaining will make them understand. My three siblings don't understand it, and we were all raised together in the same family.

Ingrid on Stormwind Farm

My wish for more pasture space can not be fulfilled, at least not at this location. Almost every available square foot is already used for that purpose. We left one acre at the front of the property unfenced. Trees and bushes will eventually form a dense noise and wind barrier. By rural standards, the traffic on our two-lane country road can be quite heavy at times. People visiting a popular farm market close to Stormwind Farm account for many of the cars driving past our land. There is easy access to highways 295 and 206. The latter traverses the state from shore points in the south all the way to the northern, mountainous regions of New Jersey. For safety reasons, I'd rather not see the alpacas graze close to the road.

Like most of southern New Jersey, our land is flat, with only the occasional gentle slope. Behind the fencing at the back of the property, the land slopes down more steeply than is usual around here. An ungrazed and unfenced buffer zone ends in a wetlands area owned by neighbors. Plenty of trees, bushes, and vines grow in this protected natural paradise and provide shelter and food for a variety of wildlife species. During late fall and winter, we can glimpse farm fields and the outline of various farm buildings through the bare trees.

The original farmhouse was built by the grandparents of our neighbor across the road. For most of the year, the only structure visible above the trees' lacy leaf patterns is the top of an old silo. We were told that dairy cows once grazed on our section of the original farm. When we purchased it, a tenant farmer had planted it in soybeans.

Because of the crops, no trees or bushes were growing on our land when we first moved here. In a way, the lack of mature trees was not all bad. We did not have to remove trees with bark or leaves that are potentially harmful to alpacas. As it is, I battle to keep the wild cherry trees from moving in and taking over. Birds drop their seeds. Once established, a wild cherry tree grows like wildfire in our soil. I planted a sycamore and maples in the pastures and dog yard. There are also pines, cedars, and a variety of spruce trees.

It's a big blessing, this rich, fertile topsoil on our land. Once we decided to breed and raise alpacas and started searching for land, I made soil quality the top priority. Regardless of good location or other desirable features, I would never have bought a farm with sandy or otherwise poor soil for our purpose. Raising pastured livestock on poor pasture land is possible but an uphill battle. It's a money pit! The prices of fertilizer and other soil amendments are high. If a farm's soil is highly suitable for pasture but has been neglected or abused, it's worth the money to fix the problems. If the soil has little humus and few minerals, I'd keep my money in my pockets.

Alpacas certainly love to graze, and their bodies are superbly designed to do so. For many months of the year, our pastures provide a tasty and nutritious mix of grasses, legumes, and beneficial herbal plants such as dandelion and plantain.

"Don't these guys ever stop?" my sister Karin wanted to know.

"Stop what?" I asked.

"Well, all I ever see them do is graze and poop," my sister reported, a little perplexed.

I laughed. Karin was visiting from her home in Germany during the height of the grazing season. The pastures were lush, the weather cool and sunny . . . so, yes, Karin was right. There was absolutely nothing else on the alpacas' minds at that time of the year than stuffing themselves with the green plants growing in such abundance.

During perfect grazing days, not one of the alpacas living on Stormwind Farm is interested in entering a barn except for a drink of water. When it's raining hard, snowing, or brutally hot, most are only too happy to seek shelter.

Our farm's two pole barns are plain but sturdy and functional. The smaller of the two measures 32 x 24 feet and houses the alpaca males. It can be entered through a service door from the dog yard as well as from one of four barn doors from the side of the pastures. On the pasture side, a tiny barn we call the Dexter House snuggles against the larger structure. It's only eighty square feet, but it's sturdy and built to last.

The barn that houses the alpaca females measures 30 x 40 feet. It also has four large doors that are opened for maximum ventilation during the summer.

Both barns have dirt floors covered with rubber horse mats. Each has a water hydrant inside and electric for lights and outlets. David did a considerable amount of work on the barns, with me acting as his helper.

To have a large building exclusively designed for storage would be nice, but I don't think it'll materialize.

"A play farm doesn't need an equipment barn," David quipped.

It's true. The small size of our farm makes large equipment financially burdensome and difficult to store. We get by very well with a good size pickup truck, a travel trailer for transporting alpacas, a golf course mower, a seed spreader, a wheel barrow, and various rakes and shovels. I use manual hedge clippers and a hand saw to trim trees and bushes.

The division of labor on Stormwind Farm is—by choice and mutual agreement—somewhat rigid. David mows, shears, and takes care of repairs that require any kind of mechanical knowledge and aptitude. He picks up supplies and transports alpacas. I take care of everything else. At times, my work includes heavy physical labor. Non-farming people often have romantic ideas about raising livestock.

"It's so beautiful on your farm," I hear from visitors.

"I feel so at peace here," my friend Mary tells me as we walk the pastures, and she admires a new cria.

Visitors rarely inquire about the work involved in running the farm. Surprisingly, that includes quite a few of the prospective breeders who come to the farm. Someone in the alpaca community coined the term "alpaca lifestyle." It drives David wild.

"It makes people think that raising alpacas means mostly leisure time and watching the grass grow," he complains whenever he hears the marketing phrase. "Nobody is telling the crop farmers that they are living the 'corn lifestyle' or the 'soybean lifestyle'."

He has a point. Come to think of it, I've never seen mention of a "cattle lifestyle" or a "goat lifestyle." It's true, there's peace and tranquility and a quiet enjoyment of all that makes up Stormwind Farm. The "alpaca lifestyle," however, also includes sweat, aching muscles, and bones deeply chilled from hours spent outdoors during a cold winter's day. Nobody should try to raise livestock on a small farm such as ours unless he or she truly enjoys the challenges of physical labor. That is, if he or she expects to make a profit.

While I perform all of the daily hard farm work, David and I annually share the labor of putting up the yearly hay supply. The hay farmer who sells us his excellent orchardgrass hay lives down the road from us. He is an important link in a whole chain of suppliers who are our local support system. We couldn't raise alpacas without the owners of stores selling seed, lime, camelid feed, rubber mats, and the many other large and small supplies that are needed on a livestock farm. We also purchase from mail order companies that offer organic products or camelid specialty items.

To my astonishment, the alpaca breeder who complained most bitterly that supplies were not readily available in his area was a visitor from Australia. Who would have thought that from the land of the thornbirds? We enjoyed the Australian's visit a great deal and spent many hours discussing alpaca farming. It was long after dinner and close to midnight when we parted.

"You invited a perfect stranger to your house for dinner?" a fellow teacher asked in alarm the next day.

Well, why not? A house is to be lived in and should be open to family as well as those who share our passions. Besides, a fellow alpaca breeder is never a stranger.

Our farmhouse, although built during the glory days of the McMansions, is of a modest size. While it boasts neither soaring ceilings nor fancy bathrooms with jacuzzis and lounging areas, it is cozy, functional, and energy efficient. There are no rooms designed, built, and decorated "for show." We live in all of them. Family and friends are always welcome. We open the farm to others by appointment. Guests who stay beyond a day or two are expected to help with chores. There's always work to do.

Of course, there's also time to rest, especially if a hard working guest helps to speed up the completion of chores assigned for the day. A favorite place to relax is our covered front porch. As porches go, it's practical rather than fancy. When my friend Marianne visited Stormwind Farm for the first time, wearing high heels and a tight skirt, she tottered up the few stairs leading to the porch and gave it a critical look.

"Not exactly what you'd find in your better gardening or decorating magazines," Marianne swiftly passed judgment on the low maintenance cement floor and three large flower pots planted with red geraniums. She wrinkled her nose at the sight of my mud encrusted farm boots. "What's this I see?" she asked in mock horror, pointing to the boots. "Those don't exactly look like the classic Wellies worn by gentle country folk."

"Oh, hush, you horrible snob," I laughed and gave her a hug.

Marianne looked around and watched the alpacas enter the lower pasture to graze. My usually talkative friend was silent for a long time. "So," she finally asked in wonder, "you are really farming?"

"Sit down," I ordered and pointed to the two comfortable rocking chairs facing the pastures. I fetched cold drinks and joined Marianne. She had already settled into one of the rockers.

Marianne and I enjoy an unusual friendship. We seldom see each other, but when we do, it always feels like we just parted mere days ago. Marianne is slim and always well groomed. Her clothes are tasteful, and her make-up is applied so expertly as to be hardly noticeable. By Marianne's standards, I am fat, and my wardrobe is a disaster. When we first met, she was appalled to discover that I owned neither lipstick nor mascara and was not familiar with any of the clothing labels she considered crucially important to know.

I was therefore not surprised when Marianne eyed the magazine I held out to her with considerable suspicion. "A fashion magazine, Ingrid?" Marianne's lips curled with open mockery.

I smiled, put the magazine in her lap, sat back, and rocked with a gentle, soothing rhythm.

This porch is worth its weight in gold, I decided with quiet satisfaction. It's a depository for my muddy boots, a drop off for parcel post when we're not home, and a shaded area to catch my breath between farm chores. Best of all, I thought, I can rock peacefully and watch my alpacas. I remembered dreaming about this before the house was even built and a single fence post had been pounded into the ground. It took years and a lot of work for my vision to become reality.

David and our nephew Jonas relax on the porch.

While Marianne read, I looked out over the farm. By now, the females and crias were spread out in the three acres making up the bottom pasture and were grazing contentedly. Black, white, fawn, brown, grey . . . what an impressive variety of fleece colors we had in our small herd! How aesthetically pleasing the alpacas looked, with their graceful bodies, expressive faces, and clean, soft fiber!

There are two distinct varieties, suri and huacaya. Their fiber characteristics set them apart. Huacaya fiber has crimp, and the fleeces have a fluffy appearance. Huacaya alpacas have a teddy bear kind of look. Suri fiber has no crimp. It's extremely lustrous and drapes down the alpaca's body in curly spirals. Suri alpacas look like sculpted art work.

We've had as many as twenty-five huacaya alpacas on Stormwind Farm. I prefer to keep the herd size around fifteen animals. That's very manageable for me and leaves me time for other pursuits such as playing with my grandchildren, writing, reading, gardening, and visiting with friends like Marianne.

Marianne! I hadn't heard a word from the old chatterbox in at least fifteen minutes. The calming motion of the rocking chair and the soothing sight of the grazing alpacas had almost lulled me to sleep. I had worked hard before Marianne's arrival and had felt a little tired.

Refreshed, I turned toward Marianne who was obviously fascinated by the contents of the magazine. "What do you think?" I asked. It was a rhetorical question. I already knew the answer.

"This is so exciting," Marianne exclaimed, pointing to a photo of a model wearing a beautiful sweater knitted from alpaca yarn. "Do you make clothing from your alpacas' hair?" Marianne asked.

"It's not called hair, it's fiber," I answered.

My friend listened intently as I talked about the history of the alpaca in its South American home lands, the well-established use of alpaca fiber by the European fashion industry, and the growing interest in alpacas and their fiber in North America. I explained how I care for the animals.

"They're so cute. Do you have to kill them to get their fiber?" Marianne asked anxiously.

"No, of course not," I answered, "they're shorn once a year." I talked about the work and skill involved in harvesting the fiber. "You're supposed to be a fashionista, Marianne," I teased, "but you've never heard of alpaca clothing?"

Marianne gave me an uncharacteristically baleful look. "Yes, I have," she protested, "my mother even had several friends who wore winter coats made from alpaca." She hesitated.

"But . . . ?" I prompted her to continue, sensing that more was to come.

"I hope you don't think I'm stupid," Marianne began again, "but I never made the connection between their coats and the animals. This visit today . . . it gives me so much to think about."

"And you haven't even left the porch yet," I teased again.

Marianne looked at the alpacas grazing in their pastures. The adults moved along slowly, their softly padded feet leaving no imprint on the vegetation. Two crias were taking turns chasing each other. A hawk flew gracefully over the males' pastures, heading toward the wetlands section with its thickets of trees and brush and the open spaces beyond. The potted geraniums bloomed in bright red profusion in their clay pots on the porch. At the entrance to one of the parking areas, the crayon yellow heads of black-eyed Susans nodded ever so slightly in the summer breeze.

"Leave this porch?" Marianne asked. "I don't think that I'll ever want to leave this porch," she answered her own question.

I leaned over and affectionately squeezed my friend's hand. "Welcome to Stormwind Farm," I said.

Breeze was sent to Serenity Alpacas to give birth to her first cria, Kalita.

Chapter 2

BREEZE AND HARLEY

The very first alpaca cria I saw was a tiny female named Carolyn. She was red with a white tuxedo pattern, only a few months old, and I tried to buy her on the spot.

"She belongs to our boarder, Tom," the farm's owners, Hugh and Carol Masters, explained.

"I'll buy her," I said.

"She's not for sale," Hugh told me.

Thirty seconds on my first alpaca farm . . . and my heart was broken. I had never, ever seen a more adorable creature in my life. David and I had bred and raised one litter of Afghan Hounds as well as several litters of Whippets. Although Whippet puppies are hellions and not to be raised by the faint of heart, all our puppies were cute. But nothing compared to this perfect, little alpaca!

"She almost looks like she's not real," I whispered to my husband.

"I know," he said and lapsed into uncharacteristic silence, a sure sign that he also was awestruck by Carolyn's beauty and seeming perfection.

We first started to inquire about alpacas in 1995. Prices paid for the animals, compared to those of other livestock such as fiber goats or sheep, were high at that time. This was simply due to the laws of supply and demand that govern a free market system. Demand was steadily growing, and supply was not keeping up. True, very few people had heard of alpacas in those days. Thanks to a great national marketing program, this was quickly changing. Breeders of llamas had paved the way, and alpacas were catching up in name recognition among the general public. The number of alpaca farms located in our home state of New Jersey was growing, but most breeders had tiny herds, and not many animals were for sale.

Our plan was to purchase a bred female and a gelding as her companion. We decided to be cautious and not commit additional funds to our new venture. A starter herd of two alpacas would have to satisfy us for the beginning. To acquire the irresistibly cute Carolyn, however, I was more than ready to throw our original purchase plan overboard without a second thought.

Carolyn was boarded at Serenity Alpacas. The New Jersey farm was beautiful and immaculate. All alpacas looked well cared-for and grazed calmly on green, spacious pastures. We had met the farm's owners, Hugh and Carol Masters, at an alpaca festival held in Pennsylvania.

Our first encounter with an alpaca breeder immediately after our arrival at the festival site had been somewhat of a shock and a disappointment. I had approached the first breeder we saw and told her about our purchase plan and budget.

The woman looked at me briefly, raised an eyebrow, and pursed her lips. "I sell only packages of four to five alpacas," she said, turned her back to me, and walked away.

"Snob!" I hissed and made a mental note to remember the face and name displayed on a tag pinned to her jacket.

Another encounter like that, and we may have left the alpaca festival to raise sheep or fiber goats. Feeling rebuffed and a little forlorn, I decided to join David. He was drinking his second cup of coffee in front of a vendor's food stand.

I already had my purse unzipped and was fishing for a dollar bill when my eyes fell on a tall, slender woman. She was leading three haltered alpacas across the festival grounds. We smiled at each other. Within a minute, Carol Masters had introduced herself, her husband Hugh, and their three alpaca males. Conversation between us flowed easily. Neither Carol nor Hugh seemed put off by our budget. They invited us for a visit to their farm. Located in Hunterdon County, a mountainous region and an easy drive from the flatlands of our South Jersey home, it had a beautiful view of the Musconetcong Valley.

We gladly accepted the invitation. The visit went well, but that day, despite my impulsive offer to purchase Carolyn, we were not ready to buy alpacas. I was sure, however, that we would return. With a last glance at Carolyn, my first alpaca love, we departed, full of excitement over what the future held for us.

The immediate future meant completing our new house on the farm. Our eight acre farm had been planted in soybeans. We had to start from scratch with all plans for a house, barns, pastures, and a dog yard. Many decisions had to be made. To save money, we acted as our own contractor. In addition to hiring subcontractors, we also put much sweat equity into building the house. Our nerves at times were stretched to a breaking point over building delays, poor workmanship, tardy deliveries, and disappearing subcontractors. Early on, I had a very small taste of what was in store for us. After only three days of working, the first set of masons left the job site to go on a hunting trip.

"I thought that is only supposed to happen in New England," I wailed.

"Guess again," our son Ben said. He seemed familiar with the recreational practices of the local trades people. "Why in the world did you start the job at the beginning of hunting season?" Ben wanted to know.

"How does he know so much about this stuff?" I asked David suspiciously.

My husband shrugged and refused to answer, leaving me to contemplate the mysterious brotherhood of men. Why did a pair of New Jersey masons feel compelled to exchange their trowels for guns in the middle of a paying job? I didn't get a chance to ask them. They upset the building inspector for some reason and were never seen again.

Every day was an adventure, none of it was easy, and we learned a lot. Finally, after two long years of hard work, the house was finished. Exhausted but also elated, we moved to the farm. The time had come to buy alpacas.

My plan was to buy the alpacas before we built a barn, put up fencing, and purchased any supplies for the animals.

"That is putting the cart before the horse," a friend warned me.

Not so! We needed guidance and advice, and I fully expected the seller of our first alpacas to be a willing mentor. Not all buyers see the wisdom in such a plan. Some pay hefty financial penalties for ignoring the importance of a mentorship.

We had stayed in touch with the owners of Serenity Alpacas. While working on the house, we had exchanged phone calls. A beautiful Christmas card arrived as well as advice on the layout of pastures and farm buildings. Until the house was completed, I had time to consider all options until we were ready to tackle those jobs. I also studied the sample sales contract Hugh had put in the mail for us.

"We don't need to look elsewhere," I told David. We had found the kind of mentors I deemed crucial for our farm's success.

Our buying trip therefore took us north again. My attention was still riveted on Carolyn. As expected, Tom could not be persuaded to part with her. It was time to forget Carolyn and move on. Hugh and Carol's own herd was small at that time. There weren't many choices, but I felt comfortable with the animals that were offered to us. We chose Soft Breeze—a black alpaca with a white tuxedo pattern—as our foundation female. She was two years old and pregnant with her first cria. In recent years, some breeders have expressed the opinion that multi-colored alpacas should not be bred. Horsefeathers! Americans, more than any other people in the world, love choices. Alpacas are the perfect fiber livestock for those who think that variety is the spice of life. They come in an astonishing array of colors and patterns.

At almost fifteen years of age, Breeze no longer produces top quality fiber. For a decade, though, her blended black and white fiber spun up into a beautiful heather grey yarn. I never had a problem selling it.

The day we signed contracts on Breeze, I also wanted to select a gelding to eventually serve as her pasture companion. My first choice was Harley, a large, coffee brown alpaca male with a small tuxedo pattern. He wasn't gelded yet, but Hugh and Carol assured us that this could easily be arranged. Harley seemed to be an easy going fellow, and his large size would allow him to serve double duty. He would be a guard animal as well as a companion.

I was very happy with my choice but didn't count on resistance from my husband. His legal name is Harley David Wood.

"No way," he protested, "we are not buying an alpaca with the same name as mine. People will think I'm so conceited that I named it after myself."

"Who cares what people think," I countered, but no amount of pleading could change David's mind.

"Forget it!" he insisted.

After some deliberation, I chose Cirrus who looked very much like Breeze. They were half-siblings, and it showed. They'd be a matching pair, I told myself. Fate intervened. Cirrus became ill and had to be euthanized shortly after we purchased him.

"Oh, this is not good," I thought, "we haven't even brought our alpacas home, and one is already dead."

Without hesitation, Hugh and Carol offered Harley as a replacement at no additional cost. We accepted. It was meant to be. Harley was ours to keep.

Six months later, barn and pastures were ready for the homecoming. Hugh and Carol transported our alpacas in the back of their van. Included in their welcoming committee was my mother who was visiting us from her home in Germany. Although she was always puzzled by my passion for farming and working with livestock, she came to enjoy watching the alpacas graze from the comfort of our front porch. Later, my mother even paid for a subscription to the German publication *Lamas* to be sent to our home.

From the very beginning, Breeze ruled the barn with an iron foot. So far, no younger female has successfully challenged her authority. Those who made any attempt to usurp the boss lady's social status soon came to regret their folly.

Generally, Breeze is a quiet ruler. She's not prone to outbursts or temperamental hissy-fits. But get her mad . . . and you better watch out! Breeze gave me a first glimpse of a temper when her first cria, Kalita, was about three months old.

Harley was the catalyst. Geldings normally lose any sexual urges, especially males that never bred a female prior to being castrated. Harley certainly never showed any interest in breeding Breeze. He seemed protective of Kalita. I happened to stand near the barn's service door one day when I saw what can only be described as a speculative look pass across Harley's face. Suddenly, he walked over to Kalita and tried to mount her. There was no mistaking his intentions. Kalita hummed nervously to her mama.

Before I could intervene, Breeze almost literally flew across the barn. Although Harley is much bigger and heavier than Breeze, she gave him a pummeling that he never forgot. With the relentless fury of an outraged mother protecting her child, Breeze not only chased him around the barn but body slammed him into the walls. My mouth dropped open as I watched. Bam . . . take that . . . bam . . and this . . bam . . and how about that . . bam! My gentle alpaca mama had turned into a lioness. Harley, his dignity destroyed, slunk out of the barn in shame and defeat. Breeze and Kalita followed. Within seconds, all three grazed peacefully as if nothing had ever happened.

Breeze has given us many babies over the years. She has always been secretive about giving birth. With our other females, there are usually subtle signs the night prior to the big event. A tail slightly raised, the choice of a different sleeping spot in the barn, repeated nibbling on flanks, a blank stare—I can often tell when a female is getting ready to give birth the next day.

Breeze hides all signs until she's in full labor. She's obviously intelligent. When we bought Breeze, Carol described her as "the Albert Einstein of alpacas," an apt description as it turned out. Many people feel that animals are not capable of using reason to think and plan ahead. How would they explain the following example of superb management of labor and birth?

One summer day, I observed Breeze lead the herd out of the barn and toward a distant pasture. I thought that was kind of odd, given the high temperature and that it happened during the hottest time of the day. Additionally, there was still plenty of good grazing left on the pasture closest to the barn. At the gate, Breeze patiently waited for me to open it and then allowed all other alpacas to pass her. That was unusual, and I wondered about what was going on. Intensely curious by now, I stood rooted to the spot and watched. Breeze lifted her head high and looked straight ahead. She looked to the right, then to the left, and finally checked out the pasture behind her. What in the world . . . ? Breeze looked straight ahead again. By now, her herdmates—excited about the new pasture— were grazing quite a distance from the gate and facing away from the barn. Suddenly, Breeze whirled around and, as fast as her big pregnancy belly allowed, ran back to the barn. Totally baffled, I followed. By the time I reached the building, Breeze stood in front of the fan and was giving birth. Quietly, I withdrew and gave her the privacy she craved. What a clever alpaca! Breeze had always given birth out in the pasture. This day, when temperatures were truly unbearable, she had arranged to have a big cooling fan all to herself.

Our Whippet, Chi-Chi, uses a similar trick when she wants me to vacate the only comfortable chair in David's office. Chi-Chi pretends to have a bathroom emergency. She frantically races between the door and the chair. "Hurry up, I practically have my legs crossed!" she barks and whines. Not wanting to risk an accidental puddle in the house, I always get up to let her out. More often than not, the little witch hops onto the chair and smugly judges me once again to be her patsy.

The herd eventually caught on to the fact that the boss lady was missing. With Harley in the lead, they went in search of her. The other females greeted the new cria, Verona, and drifted slowly back to the pasture. Harley stayed with Breeze and Verona. After his single lapse in good judgment early in his career as a companion and guard, Harley had quickly redeemed himself. Breeze and all the other females that later joined the Stormwind herd came to trust him with their crias. Our gelding's main job was to keep "his" babies safe by being alert to possible danger in and around the pastures.

Harley as a handsome, young dude

Harley carefully screened all visitors and positioned himself between the crias and strangers visiting the farm. He came to know "regulars" and learned to be more relaxed around them. He was totally devoted to the little ones. I especially remember the way this huge alpaca gelding gently play-wrestled with tiny male crias.

Harley and Breeze are still with us. They've been easy keepers, to say the least. Neither one has ever had any than routine veterinary care.

Lately, Harley is starting to show his age. He still eats well, and he's never been sick, but he's not as energetic as he used to be. When the herd grazes in the lower pasture, he often remains close to the barn now and takes a rest from his duties. Harley no longer guards the barn entrance at night. Instead, he prefers a cushier and well-protected sleeping place in the barn's interior. It's up to the mamas now to chase down naughty alpaca boys when it's time for the night's rest. When the little males disturb the peace by racing in and out of the barn a hundred times after dark, Harley lets the females deal with their juvenile delinquent sons.

He rarely intervenes now when two females get into a squabble over a flake of hay or other issues. Indignant outbursts of "I know there are other flakes of hay, but I want this one, and I was here first" from either Claudia or Sanibel no longer get a rise out of the old gelding.

I used to lock him out when I walked another male through the female pasture on its way to the breeding pen. If I didn't, Harley challenged the intruder entering his domain. Now he stays out of the way. The breeding males are young and strong. Harley knows that he no longer has the strength to prevail in a fight with them.

Soft Breeze remains spry for her age. She loves her babies. As long as she keeps up her weight and is able to nurse them, we'll let her have them. The social status of an alpaca female is very much tied to its fertility. It'll be a blow to the old herd boss when she's put out to the proverbial pasture. Breeze's fiber is still surprisingly soft, but—as is normal for old animals—there's very little staple length. Her leg coverage, never abundant, is very sparse now. This spring, I will ask my husband not to shear the fiber on her legs. If need be, we can buy a winter coat for Breeze. It'll have to be water repellent on the outside because the old girl loves to be outdoors.

In contrast to Breeze's fleece, Harley's fiber still grows long and thick. The density is probably an illusion. Our gelding's fiber is very coarse now, with lots of guard hair. Coarse fiber often gives the feeling and appearance of a much denser fleece. I simply discard the fiber of the old alpacas, and birds use it as nesting material.

We hope that Breeze and Harley can live out their lives on Stormwind Farm. While it's a little sad to see the slow decline of strength, energy, and fiber quality, it's also nice to have older alpacas like Harley and Breeze around. There's trust and understanding and a shared history. There's ease of communication and the mutual enjoyment of comfortable farm routines.

Is it financially smart to keep old alpacas around? Probably not. I say it's good for the soul. Breeders who never keep any animal long enough to reach old age on their farm don't know what they're missing. Old animals, like old people, add stability to a community. They have much to teach the youngsters in their midst. Herd animals in the wild know the importance of multi-generational living. So do the alpacas. It's only humans who have moved away from this concept and create artificial age groupings for themselves and the various generations of animals under their care. I know several alpaca breeders who—on their respective farms—maintain a separate pasture for a combined group of juvenile and yearling females. It's not something I would recommend as a routine practice. Obviously, not everyone agrees with me. Novice breeders are often confused and even irritated over the conflicting advice that is given to them.

"Not all families agree on how to raise their children," I point out. "Likewise, not all breeders agree on how to raise their alpacas."

What I try to do on our farm is to create living conditions that closely resemble those the alpacas would choose if left to their own devices. Adult female alpacas would not force juvenile and yearling females to leave the herd.

In any case, we presently have three geriatric alpacas on Stormwind Farm. David says that they are protected under Wood's Endangered Species Act. According to him, they cannot be sold or given away. Well, who's arguing?

Pearl and Riverman were never more than a few feet apart from each other.

Chapter 3

PEARL AND RIVERMAN

Although it has been a few years since Pearl first arrived at Stormwind Farm, I have not forgotten that day. She was not alone but came with her mother. Sierra was scheduled to be bred to one of our alpaca males. Pearl, a tiny cria with the occasional black spot in her lustrous white fleece, stood out among our mostly fawn, brown, and black huacaya alpacas. Riverman took one look at her and was instantly smitten. The two crias shared a pasture on Stormwind Farm for several months. In all that time, Riverman never left Pearl's side except to nurse and sleep next to his mother during the night.

If it is true that opposites attract, Riverman and Pearl were the poster children for this bit of folksy wisdom.

Riverman is the brown son of Soft Breeze, our old tuxedo-patterned herd boss. For three consecutive years, Breeze had given birth to male crias that were virtual clones of one another. Patriot, Fireman Steve, and Riverman not only looked almost identical, they were very similar in personality as well. Steady and sturdy described them best. It was easy to ignore them among their flashier-looking herdmates. By the time Sierra and Pearl arrived, Patriot and Fireman Steve had been sold, but little teddy bear Riverman had taken the place of his older siblings.

Like his brothers, Riverman always blended into the crowd. He was happy to go along to get along. Quiet and unassuming, Riverman never demanded attention, not even during or after his birth.

The day Riverman was born, my husband David and I were busy shoveling dirt to backfill a trench. The trench carried electric cable to our newly-built female barn. At noon, a light rain started to fall. At my insistence, we kept on working.

In a pasture, an open trench is a safety hazard, especially in the dark. It's true that many animals have much sharper night vision than humans. Like other prey species, alpacas typically are very aware of any changes in their environment and approach novel objects with extreme caution. Still … why take chances? I had been anxious for days to restore the pasture to a safe condition.

What particularly worried me were the daily rounds of energetic pronking. During this amazing gait, the alpacas leap forward and upward simultaneously while all four legs leave the ground at the same time. Our crias often pronk during the daytime. The adults almost always prefer to pronk at dusk or when the pastures are lit by the light of the moon and stars.

Adults as well as crias get pretty wild, overtaking and passing their herd mates as they're gamboling around and around the pasture. Miraculously, the alpacas never collide or interfere with one another in any way while they enjoy this ancient ritual.

"It's magical," a friend of mine whispered as she observed our small herd pronking silently and majestically in the dark. "It's like they're magical unicorns," she added, obviously awestruck by the performance.

I wasn't surprised by my friend's reaction. The lively and graceful pronking is truly mesmerizing and seems much like a secret celebration. I always try to observe as quietly and unobtrusively as possible.

Dusk also finds the crias chasing one another in and out of the barn in a wild game of hide and seek. The male babies especially act like little maniacs. They dodge around the cushed mamas and even leap on their backs with reckless abandon. Usually, the "reindeer games" don't stop until the mamas are fed up with their offsprings' nocturnal shenanigans and sharply call the little boys to order. The young and restless alpaca hooligans instantly transform themselves into needy babies who enjoy their last suckling of the day, and then … silence.

Between pronking and the reindeer games, there were plenty of opportunities for a lively alpaca to step into a ditch. So, no, I wasn't going to count on the alpacas' extraordinary sense of perception to prevent an accident. It was far wiser to keep on shoveling and get the ditch filled.

Pausing to rest my tired muscles, I glanced up and—"Whoa, look at Breeze!" I called to David.

Only fifty feet away from us stood Breeze, the old herd boss. Her tail was lifted, and two little feet and a head protruded from her back end. Breeze had always liked her privacy while giving birth. She often managed to keep first-stage labor signs as well as the birth itself a secret. I was mildly alarmed that she had chosen to allow us to witness the main event of her labor. Breeze could have easily given birth behind the barn without us realizing what was going on. Why the change in routine?

"Looks like we better stop," David suggested hopefully.

"No, let's continue shoveling," I countered, "we can keep an eye on Breeze while we're doing this."

All three of us worked in silence: David and I packing dirt in the trench, and Breeze pushing to expel her cria. Dangling halfway out of its mother, the cria vigorously shook its head as rain drops splashed on the tiny face. The baby was getting a shower before it was fully born! Mercifully, the rain had been reduced to a steady drizzle, and it was warm.

One more contraction, a determined push, and a wet alpaca cria wriggled on the ground! Newborn alpacas don't look like the adorable stuffed toys they resemble, once their fiber has completely dried. Right after birth, they are rather scrawny, all legs and unattractive, tiny pin heads.

I walked over to check out Stormwind Farm's newest arrival.

"It's a boy," I announced, my voice betraying my disappointment.

Instantly, I felt ashamed. Alpacas, like any other species, can produce offspring with genetic defects. This cria was obviously healthy and full of life. A birth can be difficult, with a cria lodged inside the birth canal in an abnormal position. Breeze's baby had slipped out of her as easily as a raw egg out of a cracked shell. Be happy and grateful, I admonished myself.

Focusing on the squirming newborn, I asked, "Do you think I should shut them in the barn?"

I didn't really expect an answer. David, who is content to allow me to make all decisions when it comes to the alpacas' care, knew better than to answer a rhetorical question. Ignoring me, he moved his shovel in a steady rhythm between dirt pile and trench.

Breeze would hate to be locked in a catch pen inside the barn. She loves being outdoors, and I had never confined her for an extended period of time. If I did so now, she would be very upset, possibly hysterical enough to reject her baby.

Although a gentle rain continued to fall, the air had not cooled down at all. There was no danger that the newborn cria would become chilled. Yes, I decided, mama and cria would remain with the herd.

"I'll run in the house to get Nolvasan," I announced.

"Sure," David replied, adding as if to console me, "he's a cute little guy."

After dipping the cria's navel in a small film canister filled with diluted disinfectant, I hurried back to my trench chores. By the time the task was completed, I noticed with satisfaction that the cria was walking quite steadily and had nursed several times. Breeze had always been a devoted mom with plenty of milk. No need to meddle and interfere with her mothering skills.

The soft, warm, and drizzly rain continued for three days; mother and son traveled the pasture, with Breeze grazing and the baby alternating between nursing and sleeping. Both seemed quite content.

"What's the cria's fiber like?" a friend wanted to know.

"I have no clue," I confessed and explained, "it hasn't dried yet." I told Lori that this alpaca boy seemed to like water. "If he were human, he'd make a great riverman," I laughed.

"How's the riverman?" Lori wanted to know a week later.

By that time, the cria's rich brown fiber was thoroughly dry. Far from scrawny, the little alpaca had grown into a very sturdy individual. He was adorable. The name Riverman stuck.

Riverman was adorable.

Riverman played with the other crias on the farm but did not show a particular interest in bonding with anyone but his mama. That is, until Pearl arrived—then Riverman's small world changed from one minute to the next.

Pearl was too young to be halter trained. She had to be carried out of a travel trailer alongside her mother Sierra. Once both were released inside the pasture, their owners and I stood back and relaxed. The Stormwind herd had observed the arrival of Diann, Jane, and the alpaca strangers and ventured to the front gate to greet and inspect the newcomers. With all the other alpacas swirling around, Riverman stood still as if thunderstruck. He stared at Pearl. Call it deep curiosity, instant bonding, fatal attraction, or love at first sight; I know what I saw, and it was not just, "Oh, what's that new little alpaca doing here? Another one to play with, ho hum."

Over the years, I had raised and observed enough crias to know that male alpaca crias usually prefer to play—make that wrestle and rough house—with other male crias. They will try to play with little females only if no other male close to their own size and strength is available.

Sure, they'll brazenly mount a tiny female in imitation of the matings performed by mature herd sires. Those mini-Casanovas are observant, and many know exactly what to do. Of course, their equipment isn't up to par yet — it boils down to an alpaca version of "playing doctor." Little female alpacas rarely submit to these games willingly. They are also not interested in practicing clever wrestling moves, an activity most male crias engage in with great enthusiasm. Instead, female crias usually try to spit at their tormentors or run away. Mamas intervene and chase away persistent males that refuse to take "no" for an answer from their daughters.

None of this ever happened with Pearl and Riverman. There never was any chasing, wrestling, or spitting. Instead, a gentle companionship blossomed, with the two crias hardly ever leaving each other's side. Sure, they pronked and ran after each other, but always in joyful harmony and a deep delight in each other's presence. When Pearl and Riverman became tired, they rested next to each other. They nibbled on grasses and hay side by side. The two little alpacas lightly touched noses. Standing so close together that their thighs touched, they deposited their miniscule cria pellets at the community dung pile.

Riverman gazed at Pearl with open adoration. Late in the evenings, after the herd had already retired to the barn, I would look out the living room window and often see the two crias playing outside in the dark. Their prancing, leaping, and pronking continued until one of the adults came running out of the barn and chased them inside. There were other crias to play with, but Riverman and Pearl had eyes only for each other. I sometimes wondered about the reasons for their obvious attraction to each other. They were nothing alike.

Riverman awaits Pearl's commands.

Riverman never asked to be noticed. Undemanding is not an adjective you would choose to describe Pearl. I came to learn all facets of her personality. After initially returning to Cedar Lane Alpacas in Howell, New Jersey, Pearl was later purchased by Jacalyn and Randy and boarded at Stormwind Farm. Over time, Pearl developed into the herd's busybody. Not one to be selective, Pearl minds everybody's business, including mine. No breeding occurs without Pearl sticking her head into the breeding pen to check out what's going on; no handling or training session of a Stormwind alpaca takes place without Pearl putting in her two cents. Pearl supervises my daily clean-up of dung in the pastures and makes sure that the water buckets are properly cleaned and filled. I did not become fully aware of this personality trait until Pearl and Riverman had been separated.

Jacalyn recognized early-on the special relationship between Riverman and her own alpaca. "I would love to buy Riverman," she told me, "so they can always be together."

As much as I wanted to sell Riverman to Jacalyn, I knew that this purchase would not be practical or financially sensible. Jacalyn and Randy would not own their own farm for quite some time. Additionally, by the time we discussed the subject, Riverman had already been moved to the male pasture. When young alpaca males are old enough to be weaned, it's best to remove them from the female pasture. Alpacas are induced ovulators. Unless you don't mind accidental breedings, all males must eventually be separated from females. Of course, they can be gelded, but early castration often causes health problems. Many veterinarians refuse to geld alpaca males until they are eighteen months old.

"With his gentle personality, Riverman would make a great companion gelding," I told Jacalyn, "but it doesn't make sense for you to pay boarding fees for him."

Disappointed, Jacalyn nevertheless admitted that financial prudence should override her wishes. Now was not the right time to add a male to her tiny "herd" of two females. "It doesn't seem fair to separate them," she sighed wistfully.

As weanlings, Riverman and Pearl were able to touch noses through a mesh fence but could not enjoy their previous physical closeness. Riverman was eventually sold as part of a starter herd to breeders in Maryland. The new owners took my advice and had him gelded. In a few months, Riverman will take on the job of protecting females and their crias. I am sure that he'll be perfect in that role. Pearl is still with us at Stormwind Farm.

It was a bittersweet day when Riverman left us. His departure made me once again aware of how dependent domestic animals are on the decisions and whims of their human caretakers. Livestock breeders rarely consider or even acknowledge the bonds formed between individual animals in their herds. Many people continue to deny that animals have emotions or feelings of any kind.

I don't think it's rare for alpacas to recognize former herd members many years after a separation. On Stormwind Farm, I've experienced several separations and subsequent reunions of alpacas under my care. The most dramatic involved Soft Breeze and her daughter, Kalita. One of our first sales included Kalita, her son, Columbus, and Kalita's half-sister, Verona. The latter was also Breeze's daughter but by a different sire. We had transported the small group to their new location in Bucks County, Pennsylvania. When we returned, I went straight out to the barn where the alpacas were cushed for the night. Breeze rose and looked at me expectantly.

I returned her gaze and said out loud, "I am sorry, but they are not coming back."

I felt more than a little foolish for talking out loud to an alpaca. Breeze turned away. Slowly and deliberately, she picked up a small plastic feed dish off the barn floor. Before I had the chance to react, the dish came flying through the barn and hit me hard on a thigh.

Only those who raise alpacas will appreciate how unusual—even bizarre—Breeze's behavior was that evening. Alpacas nibble on things or occasionally pick up small sticks or overturn a bucket. But this deliberate attack! That's not normal behavior for these gentle and rather shy animals. Breeze was angry, I was convinced of that! Luckily, she didn't remain angry for long.

Years later, her daughter, Kalita, returned to the farm to be bred. She had changed owners and was now very happy and content as a herd member of Alpacas of Wishing Star Hill in Bucks County, Pennsylvania. John and Kristin Thorpe are good to their alpacas and the Anatolian Shepherd dogs that guard them. When Kristin led Kalita into the lower pasture, I was preoccupied with opening and closing gates and did not pay attention to the reunion taking place between Kalita and her mother. Kristin did.

"Kalita's legs started shaking so much when she recognized Breeze, I was getting worried," she told me later.

Happy excitement or fear? I'm convinced it was the former since Kalita has always been a socially confident alpaca.

I've seen dogs tremble with excitement when they recognized their dam or siblings after years of separation. Two of our Whippets tried to nurse from their dam when they were over two years old and had not seen her since they left the farm at the age of ten weeks. With good care, alpacas can live to be around twenty-five years old. Much can happen by the time Pearl and Riverman reach that age. Who knows, maybe they will be reunited one day.

We've never had another cria romance like the one enjoyed by Pearl and Riverman. As I am writing this chapter, I look out the window and see two babies frolicking in the pasture. They were born within a few days of each other and are both roughly one month old. The female, Apple Cider, was born on Stormwind Farm. The male, Sunny, belongs to Kristin and John. His mother, Melissa, was sent here to be bred to Sure Shot's Traveling Man, one of our stud males. The first few days after Melissa and Sunny had been delivered to Stormwind Farm, Cider and Sunny spent quite a bit of time together. The cozy relationship didn't last. Sunny is no Riverman. Cider, although only a tiny tot, has the age old wisdom of all females. She quickly ferreted out Sunny's true motives for the attention he paid her. She saw lust instead of adoration and was having none of it. Sunny was firmly put in his place. Cider, all twenty-eight pounds of her, also brooks no nonsense from Pilot and Hunter, two older male crias. "Girls rule!" is Cider's message, and that's that.

*Two tough alpaca boys, Pilot and Hunter, prefer the
outdoors to seeking shelter in their barn.*

Chapter 4

ALPACA BOYS

In the South American homelands of the alpaca, males are called machos. I thought a while about changing the title of this chapter but then decided against it.

Here at Stormwind Farm, we've always called our males "the boys." The building that houses them is "the boy barn." This in no way is meant to insult and diminish their maleness and virility. Rather, it's a sign of our affection for the male population of our farm's small alpaca community.

Many livestock breeders think of the males born on their farms as nothing more than a necessary evil. Courtesy of artificial insemination, breeders of dairy cows or cattle have little or no need to house and feed even one sperm producer. Sperm can conveniently be purchased in "straws" from breeders who specialize in that aspect of livestock reproduction. Since males are not needed and are often a nuisance, most are slaughtered when they reach a weight to make it profitable.

On Stormwind Farm, we don't slaughter, and we don't practice artificial insemination. Like other breeders with small herds, limited acreage, and modest advertising budgets, we hope for the birth of female alpacas. Females usually sell for higher prices than males. Not surprisingly, successfully promoted males with high national profiles can fetch enormous prices at times. Campaigning an alpaca male on the show circuit is very expensive and time-consuming. Our farm's program doesn't fit that niche. Our home-bred males sell inexpensively as junior herdsires, fiber males, or companion geldings. Of course, buyers may show the alpacas they purchase from us. All our stock is registered and eligible to be exhibited in shows sanctioned by the *Alpaca Owners and Breeders Association* (AOBA). I limit our own farm's show schedule to an inexpensive Level I show each year.

On most alpaca farms, a newborn male cria is rarely considered cause for celebration. Family and fellow breeders usually respond to the announcement of its birth with a rather lame and falsely cheerful, "Well, as long as it's healthy."

I would like to say that we're different. We're not. It is simply an economic fact that our farm account will be healthier with the birth and eventual sale of a female. That's too bad. Truth be told, many alpaca males are far more endearing and lovable than most alpaca females.

Recent visitors to Stormwind Farm were mesmerized and highly entertained by our young males, Pilot and Hunter. As they watched the crias wrestle, flip, and race each other around the pasture, husband and wife laughed out loud.

"These two are really something," the woman exclaimed, "they're hilarious!"

"We had no idea that alpacas have such personalities," the man added.

I expected this comment because I hear it often from visitors who walk our pastures. People rarely view herd animals as individuals with very distinct personalities. I was guilty of that. In my pre-alpaca days, I never expected to recognize such a variety of personality traits among herd members. The entertainment value of grazing fiber producers totally took me by surprise. The boys on our farm are all different. Their differences extend beyond conformational and fiber properties.

For example, Pilot and Hunter have been easy to handle and train, but they're physically tough boys. Although they have the Dexter House to shelter them from rain and snow, Pilot and Hunter prefer to stay outdoors. I was worried about them during the last snowstorm. My worries stopped when I saw them cushed behind a high snowdrift. Their beautiful fiber crusted over with snow, the two alpacas were placidly chewing their cud. They seemed quite content.

As in most species, mamas can have a great influence on their sons' behavior, at least while the boys are young. For example, Breeze's boys are always well-behaved. She simply will not tolerate bad manners. She keeps close tabs on her offspring. At the same time, she allows her sons enough freedom to learn how to fit in with herd mates and interact with humans.

Not all alpaca males enjoy the benefit of being raised by such a wise mama. Claudia's son, Rupert, comes to mind. Poor Rupert! He was hardly ever allowed to play with the other boys and explore the pasture without close adult supervision. Crias that tried to entice Rupert to join them were chased away by his overprotective mama.

A few steps too many away from Claudia, and it was always, "Rupert, get back here. Those are not nice children."

When it was time to deliver Rupert to his new home, I feared for his safety. "Rupert is a bit of a sissy. He's never been in a play fight. I'm afraid he won't know how to defend himself," I told Jim, his new owner.

I needn't have worried. There was a happy bounce to little Rupert's steps when I led him out of the pasture and into our travel trailer. Rupert never once glanced back at his domineering mother. He's been fine at Jim's farm and learned quickly to hold his own with the other males.

In a small herd, it sometimes happens that only a single male is born during a year of otherwise all female births. Of course, breeders are ecstatic when this occurs. We must pity the little male singleton. Without a playmate to join in rough and tough games, it wanders the pastures with little to do. Trouble is its middle name.

Two years ago, we were blessed with the birth of several females. Things were calm and orderly in the pastures and the barn. A little boring, to be sure, but in this case boredom wasn't so bad. The arrival of Kalita with her baby, Greyson, enlivened things considerably. Greyson, as his name implies, is a beautiful silver grey alpaca male. What a character and ham he was while staying with the herd at Stormwind Farm!

For Greyson, every day was an adventure to be lived to the fullest. One night, as I walked to the barn for bed check, a terrible storm broke out. I have never feared thunder and lightning. Alpacas also don't seem to be very sensitive to any noise related to storms, but this particular storm presented extreme conditions.

The alpacas had barely reached the safety of the barn when the first lightning bolt zigzagged through an eerily lit up sky. It was followed by a deafening clap of thunder. After securing the barn doors, I switched my attention to the alpacas. As thunder and lightning followed each other at regular intervals, the alpacas remained frozen in fear. Nobody moved; nobody chewed cud. Most were cushed, but several females and Harley remained standing, as motionless as statues. Not so Mr. Greyson. The impish tyke was having the time of his life. A clap of thunder and a quick slalom around Claudia and Melissa . . . wheee! A bolt of lightning, another clap—how about a leap over Caramel? Yippee! This was fun, fun, fun!

Greyson figured out soon enough that his wild antics were not met with the customary disciplinary measures, not even from Grandma Breeze. One more rumble—a leap over Memphis and old Grandma at the same time? No problem! How about a twist in midair, followed by a kick with all feet off the ground? Weird how the females are all just cushed or standing around. What's wrong with them? Who cares? Life is grand and to be celebrated.

What a performance! First I laughed, then I quickly covered my face with my hands. "Oh God, I hope he doesn't break a leg or his darn little neck," I worried. What would I tell Kristin and John, his owners?

Mercifully, lightning and thunder were soon followed by a silent sky and then a torrential downpour. The latter cleared the air, and calm returned to Stormwind Farm.

On some farms, the atmosphere in the alpaca male quarters is anything but calm. Over the years, I've analyzed the reasons for the mayhem in these herds and try hard to prevent problems with our own animals. We presently house five adult males in the "boy barn." They lead a mostly peaceful existence. There are several reasons for this.

One is our plentiful pasture. If idle hands are the Devil's workshop for humans, idle mouths lead to boredom and fights among alpaca males. Keep them busy grazing, and they won't have time for confrontations.

Another reason for our peaceful male kingdom is the spacious barn. During inclement weather, the boys are not forced to sit "cheek to cheek." If little disagreements flare up, the two combatants are able to move away from each other and thus avoid a serious fight.

There is a third reason: The males leave their own domain to breed. Each male is thereby forced to accept the barn and the pasture not as its personal fiefdom but as community space to be shared peacefully with others. On farms where females are brought to a male pasture or barn for breeding, alpaca males can become very territorial. The fighting can become so ferocious that one or several males may need their own private pasture and barn space. I don't want such a situation on our farm. Our infrastructure could not accommodate it in any case. It's best to use preventive measures.

Finally, maybe the most important factor in promoting harmony is Tasman, the most dominant male on Stormwind Farm. He earned this honor by the sheer force of his personality. Many people are under the misconception that the dominant male in a herd is the one starting all the fights to prove it's the boss. That's not how male hierarchies work in a closed herd. Once a male has firmly established its dominance, it doesn't need to fight. Tasman certainly doesn't.

Cherry Ridge Tasman

When I bought him as a young male from my friend, Pat Craven of Cherry Ridge Alpacas, she told me, "Tasman is a caretaker. He watches over all the other animals."

At the time, I thought Pat anthropomorphized just a bit too much. I owe Pat an apology because she was absolutely right and very observant to have picked up on this character trait.

Unless the weather is really nasty, Tasman elects to remain outside, day or night. Come nightfall, he positions himself so that he can see what's going on inside the male barn and keep an eye on the females as well. One fine day, Tasman was standing close to the female pasture. On the other side of the fence, Sanibel was cushed with Hunter. The cria was only a few hours old. Summer rains in New Jersey can be sudden and heavy. That day, the skies darkened suddenly and opened seemingly without warning.

All females, crias, and Harley rushed into the barn. Sanibel hesitated a few seconds, then thought, "To heck with the baby." She made haste to follow the herd.

The poor cria was left in the heavy rain all alone. Tasman was beside himself with worry. He paced and cried and carried on so fiercely that I thought, "I'll see my first alpaca have a heart attack any minute." Tasman did not calm down until he saw me scoop up Hunter and carry him into the barn.

Fortune and Traveling Man are the only males that occasionally engage in fairly serious fighting. Fortune, our black halter show champion, is an extremely mild-mannered male. It's always the larger T-Man that instigates the fights. T-Man stands out among the other males because of his very lustrous, white fiber. While Fortune and T-Man try to pin each other to the ground, Tasman grazes. His status is secure. There's no reason to join the fray.

Old Dexter keeps a low profile. Like Harley, he knows that he is vulnerable because of his age. He takes great care not to provoke the other males. When they gather at the fence line to check for open females, Dexter discreetly remains in the vicinity of the barn. He's the wise, old man of the group. When herd dynamics call for it, I ask the mahogany-red Dexter to be the mentor for one or several weanling males.

Prince is the youngest of the breeding males, and I hope to "start" him with a female this spring. He grew up under Dexter's guidance.

Dexter obviously was a good teacher because Prince is extremely respectful and deferential toward the older males. Of course, he's still very young. He may start to challenge his pasture mates as he matures. Occasionally, Fortune or T-Man will engage Prince in a wrestling match. It's pretty obvious they don't consider him serious competition. He's the younger kid brother. As long as he acknowledges their dominance over him, they'll give him a few minutes of good-natured play-fighting when they feel like it.

I've made an interesting observation over the years. People who don't own alpacas will find my conclusion hard to believe. It's happened too many times, though, to be a coincidence. My alpaca males show off for human female visitors! I know it sounds bizarre, but I'm convinced that it is true. Weeks can go by without a single fight. Let a woman, especially a young one, visit the farm, and a fight breaks out. Even Tasman and Dexter will get into the act at times.

Alpaca males have fighting teeth that must be filed to prevent serious injuries. This sounds ominous and very dangerous, but it's not nearly as bad as it sounds. The procedure needs to be done only twice during a male's lifetime. David and I take care of it ourselves. While the filing of fighting teeth prevents injuries, only the other smart management practices I mentioned ensure tranquility in the male pastures and barns.

"This all sounds so ridiculous," one prospective buyer told me when I explained my management system and the reasons for it. "I'll not play psychologist to a bunch of alpacas," he added contemptuously.

Remaining silent, I looked at Tasman observing us curiously and intently from a distance. Fortune and T-Man were grazing companionably side by side. Initially interested in the visitor, Prince and Dexter had turned their attention to one of the forsythia bushes I had planted near the fence. They were busy pruning the branches that had grown through the wire mesh into the pasture.

Halter Champion Bella Cria's Good Fortune

Psychologist? I was disappointed in myself. I had obviously not done a good job explaining the reasons for my management choices. They are all about understanding and respecting the unique physical and emotional needs of a specific species. In South America, wild camelids like the vicuña travel in herds made up of females and crias. Each herd is protected by a territorial male. As young males become sexually mature, they are driven away by the male that guards and breeds the females. They join bachelor herds until they are strong and bold enough to wrest away their own little herd from an old or sickly male. Vicuñas are the ancestors of our alpacas. Their instincts are still very much present in their domesticated cousins.

It's not normal herd behavior for several mature camelid males to live together, but that's reality on a North American breeding farm. Why shouldn't I do everything to prevent tension from building up in the male pastures?

I know that our alpaca males enjoy one another's company, despite their occasional fisticuffs. Fortune and T-Man are especially close to each other. I don't recall the reason, but I once separated them into adjoining pastures. They stopped almost all grazing and spent hours cushed side by side, with only the wire fence between them. After a few days of watching this pathetic state of affairs, I moved both back into the same pasture.

Sure Shot's Traveling Man

I love spending time with the animals I call "my boys." They're easy to handle and comfortable to be with at all times. Of course, they don't obey me the way trained dogs will follow commands. I don't deceive myself into thinking that they crave my attention.

Still, they're my pasture companions, and they treat me with respect. I can accidentally brush against their rear ends without fear of being kicked. Although the males may become upset and even angry when a pregnant female "spits off" during a behavior test, I need not worry that they will direct their anger at me. How nice to be able to enter the male pastures at any time—day or night—without fear of being tackled, gored, chased, rammed, bitten, or kicked! That includes breeding season, which lasts from spring to late fall on Stormwind Farm.

I understood early on that communicating with our alpacas is important if I wanted to earn their trust. With the boys, that means occasionally walking up to them in the pasture and forcing them to vacate their space for me. I manage this without touching them. Why do I do this? Because I can! It's the language of herd animals, and one that the alpacas understand. It's the language that has earned me their respect.

Unlike horses, alpacas are rarely physically affectionate with other herd members. They don't groom or touch one another in a loving way. Mamas, very young crias, and nanny alpacas are the exception, but these exceptions only confirm the rule. Some breeders advertise alpacas as a "huggable investment." This particular marketing slogan makes me very unhappy. Alpacas don't like to be hugged. A quick hug now and then will be forgiven, but frequent hugging and handling can have very unpleasant repercussions.

Alpaca crias that are *extensively* handled and hugged by humans often turn into aggressive and unmanageable adults. The adorable fleecy playthings morph into potentially dangerous individuals. This is especially true of males. Alpaca females that are extensively handled as crias may also become pushy and hard to handle as adults. Prospective alpaca owners— even people who already own alpacas— are often aghast when confronted with the sad facts.

One new owner who visited Stormwind Farm started crying, "But how can that be possible? You mean I can't play with the babies?" Her eyes overflowed with tears. "Why didn't anybody tell me?" she demanded accusingly.

I didn't know who the "anybody" was that she referred to. On Stormwind Farm, we *do* tell our customers to keep their loving hands off young crias as much as possible. It's the main reason that I don't halter train alpacas until they're at least six months old.

My visitor's horrified reaction was understandable. Her obvious ignorance of alpaca behavior was not her fault. Most people are several generations removed from farm life and daily exposure to livestock. How would they know that not only alpaca males but also rams, bucks, bulls, and the males of many other prey species become dangerous with time if imprinted on humans as youngsters?

"What about all those farm animals in 4-H shows? They're handled a lot as babies. What about them?" my visitor had demanded to know through her tears.

They're slaughtered long before they reach sexual maturity and with it the danger point. Those that are spared injure plenty of people, including children, if given the chance. Wise livestock owners take precautions. For example, some rams wear ram shields not as a fashion statement or just to stop them from fighting with a rival.

Our visitor was too overwrought to stay long enough to hear the good news. If an alpaca male is properly raised—that means raised by an alpaca mama—it is easily trained after weaning. With good management, it'll be a perfect gentleman. Plenty of small children safely exhibit adult alpaca males in various show venues and have success and fun doing so.

The only male on our farm that has a bit of a behavioral issue is Prince. He was very focused on people when he arrived on Stormwind Farm as a youngster. I've managed to do considerable damage control so far. Prince is never handled unless it's absolutely necessary. Visitors may not touch Prince to inspect his fiber. He's received more than a few harsh taps on the nose when he invaded my space. At least once a day, I purposely and quite deliberately force Prince to move out of the space he occupies in the pasture. I do not touch Prince when I do this. I don't need to.

He understands my message: "In the pasture hierarchy, I rank higher than you do. Don't challenge me."

"He's a stalker!" Maria complained jokingly.

Visiting our farm for a long weekend, she enjoyed helping care for the alpacas. I explained that she must firmly reject Prince's pleas for her attention and demonstrated what she must do to discourage Prince from crowding her and trying to establish his dominance over humans.

The other boys also help. Tasman often chased Prince away from me when I verbally expressed my annoyance over Prince's inappropriate behavior. Things have much improved since then, but there is obviously still room for progress. Prince's realization that I am not his playmate does not automatically transfer to other people. Each person who comes in contact with him will have to face the issue all over again. Prince is a stunningly beautiful male. I intend to use him at stud. Luckily, his behavior issue is not something that he will pass on to his offspring.

A friend with no livestock experience recently bought a flock of sheep.

"The ram is so cute and friendly," she enthused. "He comes and rubs his head against my legs and likes to have his back scratched," the praise continued.

I hesitated. Not everybody wants or appreciates unsolicited advice. This time, however, my friend's safety was at stake.

"Here's what you should know . . .," I began to explain.

*Dual Champion Stormwind's No No Josette, FCH was the
first puppy born under the Stormwind prefix.*

Chapter 5

STORMWIND WHIPPETS

The only animals sharing the house with us are our Whippets. A dog played an important part in our lives long before David and I married in 1970 in a small German village. The dog's name was Tanjuk von der Irminsul. He had been bred and was sold to us by Frau Else Spiegel, a well-known German breeder. "That's how it all started," I tell people who inquire how we came to breed alpacas.

Oddly, David and I were both raised by mothers who did not permit their children to own dogs. David's father, who agreed to allow the children to have a dog, was overruled by Mrs. Wood. My own dad was born and grew up on a farm and thought of dogs as respected working partners, not coddled house pets. At least the Wood family had a cat.

I met David while he was stationed in Germany as an airman in the US Air Force. He told me about his parents and three siblings. I was curious to see what they looked like. I had to wait several years to find out. In Germany, David only carried a photo of one family member in his wallet. It was a snapshot of Dolly, the cat. Dolly lived to a ripe, old age. She was still alive when we arrived in the United States with ten dollars in our pockets and an apricot-colored Afghan Hound, Tanjuk, at our heels. They represented the sum total of our possessions.

Years later, my husband was to claim that he had unleashed a monster when he bought Tanjuk from Frau Spiegel. It's true, I was bitten by the breeding bug early on, but our one and only litter of Afghan Hounds almost derailed my early passion. Afghan Hounds are lovely and very interesting dogs. Because most have no guard hair, their silky coats form dense mats unless they're brushed out on an almost daily basis. An enormous amount of time had to be devoted to our dogs' grooming. We could not afford to pay to have this done. The many hours spent brushing and bathing the dogs squashed any desire I had to make breeding quality Afghan Hounds my mission in life. I did not enjoy the grooming, and we eventually clipped their gorgeous coats to save my sanity.

By the time our son, Ben, was born in 1976, we still owned several Afghan Hounds. In 1978, we added a Whippet to our family. Pippet the Whippet had been given to me as a gift by a breeder who lived in Florida and had traveled to New Jersey to judge a lure coursing trial. For Ben, who remained an only child, the dogs were company and playmates.

A few years later, my son accompanied me to a small hobby kennel in New Jersey to look at a brindle and white Whippet puppy. We wanted a bitch, and Bibi was the only girl in the litter. Ben and I both fell in love with her lively, outgoing personality and flashy markings.

After our last Afghan Hound died of old age, I bred Bibi. Over several decades, I bred four litters of Whippets. Each time, I retained one or two puppies for our own enjoyment. The others were placed in carefully chosen homes. Only once did I make an error in judgment. Luckily, the puppy was returned to me, and I was able to find new owners. I know where all the dogs are that I've bred over the years and will feel responsible for them to the end of their lives.

Raising Whippet puppies was a lot of work. The first four weeks were always easy because the mamas took great care of their babies. Then the hard work began. We have a tiny kennel with an attached run in the dog yard. Puppies and their dam were moved to these quarters at the beginning of the fifth week. Once outdoors, the puppies—far from forgotten or neglected—were played with and allowed to leave the run under supervision to explore the much larger yard. They were fed, watered, cooled down in hot weather, de-wormed, and inoculated. Many tiny nails had to be clipped each week.

The adults were much easier to care for. In contrast to Afghan Hounds, Whippets are wash-and-wear dogs. Freed from hours of laborious brushing and bathing, I had time to become more involved in lure coursing and racing. Unlike thousands of unfortunate racing Greyhounds, no Whippet is ever euthanized because it is too slow on the coursing field or on the track. To the contrary, some of the clubs with which I've been involved sponsor a special *Turtle Trophy* and award it to the slowest racer of the day. It's a mission statement of sorts: "Our dogs are family members. They don't have to be fast for us to love them." Winners of the trophy took to proudly wearing *Fear the Turtle* t-shirts.

There were no monetary rewards. The owners of winning dogs took home dog dishes, dog toys, and other trinkets as prizes. That is still true today.

My sister-in-law Barbara once shook her head, "Why do you do all this work for a dish towel with the picture of a rabbit on it?"

It was all about the dogs. Whippets *love* to chase things. They don't care if the "bunny" is a piece of fake fur with a plastic "screamer" inside. Likewise, owners didn't care about the financial or social status of other Whippeteers. Our "regulars" ranged from wealthy hobbyists to people who could barely afford the travel expenses and very modest entry fees. Respect was given to those who bred or trained good dogs, regardless of what they did in their private lives. Within months of her permanent disappearance from the sport, hardly anyone remembered the name of the beautiful model who arrived at several race meets over the span of one year. Her chauffeur always looked utterly bored over the prospect of another day spent in the rural hinterlands of New Jersey. In contrast, almost everybody remembered the names of the great racing dogs and the owners who loved them, long after the dogs had been retired from the track.

Owners took excellent care of their dogs, at home as well as at race meets. When a genetic defect (bully gene) surfaced in the breed, most breeders did not hesitate to take advantage of genetic testing.

Politics are played in all organizations. Whippet racing politics were no exception. Things got pretty wild and wooly sometimes. Passion ran deep for the sport of racing and the dogs themselves. At times, that passion was expressed in a less than gentlemanly or ladylike manner. There'd be screaming matches and, although rarely, demands to settle an argument with a fist fight.

Overall though, the racing crowd was a small, close-knit, and highly social group. Frequent parties were loud and featured lots of good food. I was once voted into a club because "she makes a good apple cake." This announcement was followed by a rowdy chorus of yeahs and wild applause. Most parties were held at a large house owned by club members. We called it the *Ponderosa* after a ranch featured in the television show *Bonanza*. The owners permitted guests to bring their dogs in the house. Rooms filled with talking, laughing, drinking, eating, and arguing owners were further crowded by the horde of Whippets that frolicked in all possible locations, stole food from the buffet, and sometimes lifted their legs on a couch.

No doubt, the owners of racing Whippets were a colorful bunch. Some would have raised eyebrows in a socially conservative neighborhood. The Whippeteers took the presence of these rather eccentric individuals in their stride. One of the oldest and most successful North American Whippet breeders was rumored to have worked as a prostitute in her younger days. I don't know how she supported herself in her old age. When I met her, she and her Whippets lived in a small caretaker apartment on a large estate. Quite a large percentage of the racing stock at that time traced back to her breeding lines. Her knowledge of pedigrees and training methods was generally acknowledged as superior to that of many other breeders. The information about her previous source of income was only mentioned in passing.

Years later, when I had sent one of Bibi's grandsons to a new home, I revealed the colorful and "racy" background of his distant ancestral line to the new owner.

"My goodness, that's really something," the shocked woman exclaimed. Then she whispered into the phone, "Don't worry, the puppy will never be told. It could give him a complex."

I never knew whether she was kidding or serious, and I thought it best not to ask.

When I was given my first Whippet, I never dreamed that my hobby of breeding "the poor man's race horse" would lead to our purchase of a farm and the breeding of alpacas. There is a long history of farming on both sides of my family, with crops as well as with livestock. One of my cousins still farms the family's vineyards in Germany's beautiful and romantic Mosel valley. Growing wine never interested me. I far preferred cows and sheep and the pastures they grazed on. Collecting eggs with my grandmother, Maria, watching my grandfather, Anton, care for his bees, and raking hay with my great-aunt, Rosa, made me happy. I envied Johanna Spyri's *Heidi* and her life in the Swiss Alps.

As a teenager, I spent hours reading my maternal grandmother's romance novels. Grandmother Helene never farmed in her life, but the novels invariably featured passionate tumbles in the hay between good looking, muscular farm boys and the pretty girls who worked in barns and fields. My father, who disapproved of my grandmother sharing this reading material with me, said it was all a bunch of nonsense. Hay was itchy, he commented dryly one day, and any farm boy would know better than to have sex in a hay loft with his girl. Children were not so bold then as they are today, and I never asked the obvious question.

After David and I moved to the United States, I found out quickly that my husband had no intention of ever tumbling in a hay loft, not even in a moment of passion. Quite frankly, he had no interest in doing anything with, in, or on top of hay. I was to discover later that he didn't know the difference between hay and straw and was totally unconcerned over this glaring lack of knowledge.

His ancestors included a policeman, yacht builders, teachers, and engineers. If a farmer had been among them, his or her genes had obviously been lost to the present generation. No wonder that David considered my preoccupation with "digging in the dirt" rather strange and resisted the purchase of any property larger than half an acre.

My longing for a farm with livestock never ceased, but I slowly accepted what couldn't be changed. I couldn't breed sheep, goats, or cattle, but I could breed Whippets.

In my opinion, dogs should never be bred commercially. Ethical breeders rarely make a profit. Most are lucky to break even. Breeding Whippets was a hobby, but one that I took seriously. David was puzzled by the many hours I spent poring over pedigrees, reading books on dog care and genetics, and handling or training the dogs in our household. More than once, he commented on what he considered an inordinate amount of time spent on chores without a profit to show for my labor.

"Why don't you find animals to breed that can make money?" he asked repeatedly. "How about horses?" he suggested at one time.

I had no interest in horses other than to admire their beauty from a distance. The books about horses that I borrowed from the local library quickly educated me about the complexity of the horse industry. Very few people make money in horses. Getting into any kind of business in the equine field usually calls for an enormous financial investment. With my limited financial resources, it would take years to acquire enough knowledge and resources to become a successful horse breeder.

Livestock such as sheep, goats, and cows did not appeal to David. "They'll have to go to slaughter," he pointed out, "and I don't want to go there."

"Hypocrite," I accused him, knowing that he enjoyed a good steak as much as the next person.

My dream of ever owning and living on a farm seemed impossible to become reality. A few months after another conversation on the subject had ended in a stalemate, an idle search through the county library's livestock section ended with my discovery of *Llamas for Fun and Profit*. Dinner was not served in the Wood household that night. Always a voracious reader, I devoured the book in one sitting from cover to cover.

More astonishing discoveries were in store for me that evening. Our son, Ben, worked for a farmer during his summer vacations. One of their hay customers was a local llama breeder! I had not known this and now prodded Ben for more information. After I shared what I had learned about llamas with David, the question I posed to him did not hold any real hope for an answer that would make me happy.

"Will you buy a farm with me if I can raise llamas?" I wanted to know.

"Yes," David answered.

I was speechless for only a brief moment. Before David could change his mind, I said firmly, "Tomorrow, I'll make an appointment to visit the llama breeders."

I felt elated. David looked a little doubtful.

"Once we have everything ready to go, you won't have to do a thing but sit on the porch in a rocking chair," I solemnly promised.

It was the biggest lie I ever told in my life. At the time, I believed it myself.

The search for llamas led to alpacas. Their smaller size and end product—their fiber—were the deciding factors. Although many llamas are currently bred for superior fiber, the large framed, old-fashioned pack llama is making a strong comeback. There are also miniature llamas.

As I became more active in breeding, raising, and selling alpacas, the Whippet activities had to be curtailed. My mother always reminded her children, "You can't dance at two weddings at the same time." My days of racing and breeding Whippets are over, and I've accepted their loss. That doesn't mean that I don't miss them. I am deeply appreciative of what I learned during that time.

Breeding and racing Whippets did not begin to teach me all I needed to know about raising alpacas. My years with Whippets nevertheless prepared me for breeding and raising alpacas in many important ways. They taught me patience and resilience. I learned to be physically and mentally tough and to square my shoulders in the face of disappointments. I came to realize that the breeding and selling of animals is an emotional roller coaster. Much can be controlled but not everything. My powers of observation increased tenfold over my years caring for Whippets. So did my recognition that meticulous attention to details leads to the road called success. Being active in various sighthound clubs taught me terrific organizational skills. I didn't know it at the time, but I had a free education as an event planner. Thanks to the Whippets, my alpaca learning curve has been far more gentle than that experienced by many other breeders.

Our current Whippet population consists of three bitches. There are the old litter sisters, Rainy and Chi-Chi, Bibi's granddaughters. Their mother, Stormy, gave birth to them in a litter box set up in our farm kitchen. As youngsters, they loved to run and play all day in their large, fenced play yard. They chased rabbits, groundhogs, and field mice. Quite often, they sent stern messages to the deer to keep their distance from the property line. Those days are gone. Now that Rainy and Chi-Chi are old, they prefer to stay in the house most of the time.

Ingrid's friend, Kristin, plays with Chi-Chi in the fenced Whippet yard.

Our youngest and third Whippet is a very fast bitch named Stormwind's Turbo Diesel. Her mother, Ariel, is a litter sister to Rainy and Chi-Chi. I feel a little sorry for Diesel because she should have another young dog to play with her. She's super affectionate and craves attention. On warm days, I often see her lying in the grass on her back, all four legs straight up in the air, staring at the sky. What can she be thinking?

Although Whippets and alpacas don't share living space, they interact with one another. Our dog yard shares a fence line with one of the male alpaca pastures. Whippets and alpacas occasionally touch noses. Diesel acts tough and orders the alpacas to keep their distance. The old girls sometimes still bark ferociously when the males approach the fence. The alpaca boys are convinced that it's all bluff and pretentions and pay little heed to Diesel's hysterics and the old girls' feeble posturing. Most times, the members of each species ignore the other group and simply go about their own business. The alpacas graze, and the Whippets patrol the yard. Regardless, I prefer to keep alpacas and Whippets at a safe distance from one another. A sighthound's instinct to chase is extremely strong. A kick from an alpaca could easily injure a small, elderly Whippet. In any case, Rainy has become blind and needs protection.

Over the last few years, the Whippets' world has diminished in scope. They no longer travel in pursuit of the fake bunny. I don't think they're unhappy. There are live bunnies to chase, holes to dig next to the burning bush growing near the kitchen window, and groundhogs to bark at as they steal our neighbor's tomatoes. Birds bear watching. There are alpacas to kiss or to lecture about respecting property lines. The deer patrol is a never ending chore. Cats need to be warned away and voles killed before they have a chance to slip back into their earthen tunnels. There are visitors to greet and owners to be snuggled with.

It's a rich and fulfilling life. If you asked the Whippets, they'd probably say, "We are content." Stormwind Farm is their home.

Eagle

Chapter 6

Eagle and Triton

Eagle was Claudia's first cria. His birth would have been considered uneventful except for his unusual behavior right after being born. A major Whippet distraction added to the excitement.

Unlike alpacas, which are induced ovulators, bitches come into heat at more or less regular intervals. Usually, it's once or twice a year. Many dog breeders have their veterinarians perform tests to pinpoint ovulation and with it the best day for a successful mating. I prefer to go the natural route. It involves observing the change of the vulva for clues and then giving the stud two or three opportunities for fertilization. This has worked just fine for me.

The year of Eagle's birth, I had decided to breed Ariel. The black and white bitch is a full sister to Rainy and Chi-Chi. I co-own her with my long-time friend, Marie. The plan was for Ariel to whelp and raise her puppies on Stormwind Farm. My selected sire, Natron, was an incredibly fast racing Whippet with a wonderful temperament.

Finally, the long awaited day had arrived! Marie drove down to the farm, with Ariel tucked safely inside her traveling crate. Eager to leave as soon as she got there, my friend sat on the edge of a rocking chair on the front porch. She was ready to depart for the scheduled breeding at the home of Shoreline Whippets, a small hobby kennel just like ours. Natron and his owners were expecting us.

"Wait, I'll just have to get my pocketbook, and then we can leave," I told Marie, throwing an anxious glance at the small herd of alpacas grazing in the pasture closest to the house.

Claudia had shown several signs of impending birth since last night. Not the best timing, that was for sure. I took a closer look and—there was no mistaking Claudia's raised tail. She held it out as stiff and straight as a flag pole. That could only mean one thing: It's cria time!

"Marie, you are about to witness the birth of an alpaca. Sit back, have another cigarette on the porch, and enjoy the show," I announced, trying to sound cool and unconcerned.

This was Claudia's first baby. Who knew what could happen? My friend was not impressed.

"Well, as long as my Ariel gets bred today, and I can drive home before it gets dark, it's fine with me," Marie replied. She asked with some suspicion, "How long will this take?"

"Oh, not that long," I purposely answered rather vaguely, not revealing that it can take up to two hours for a cria to get up on its feet and start nursing.

That time frame didn't include the thirty minutes that are not unreasonable for the second stage of labor.

"O.K., let the show begin." Marie settled in a porch chair, clearly expecting instant action.

I rushed into the pasture for a closer look. There—two legs and the head were already out, a contraction, another one a few minutes later— soon I was inspecting a fawn colored alpaca male cria. It was breathing and seemed very alert. The herd gathered around to check it out. Marie applauded from the porch. So far, so good. With some luck, we'd be able to leave the farm in another hour. David could be left in charge of making sure that Claudia had passed her placenta, but I wanted to see for myself that the cria was getting nourishment. First time moms can be a little reluctant to allow nursing.

With my back to Claudia and the newborn, I turned toward Marie. "Now you've seen an alpaca birth," I stated rather superfluously, raising my voice across the pasture. "Hopefully, we can—"

Marie's loud laughter interrupted my promise that Ariel would be bred today. I looked around to see where she was pointing. What I saw astonished me. Normally, it takes a while for a newborn cria to adjust to life on "the outside." Sometimes, its lungs are a little congested. It struggles repeatedly to get on its feet and stumbles around in an attempt to find its mother's teats. Some crias get so tired out from all this hard work that they cush to rest, only to try again fifteen minutes later. That's all very normal and no cause for concern.

I would have believed another breeder to be guilty of vast exaggeration or outright fibbing if I had been told Eagle's story. Newborn alpaca crias simply do not rise within seconds of their birth and walk across a large pasture; except Eagle did! The entire herd followed him as if taking part in a festive parade, with the cria acting as the parade's marshall. Marie, who was accustomed to newborn puppies lined up like little loaves of bread against their dam, was in stitches. I was speechless.

When Eagle's birthday parade was stopped by the pasture fence, he turned around and walked back to the spot where he had been born. Within minutes, Eagle was nursing, and Marie, Ariel, and I were heading to our Whippet tryst.

"Wow, how exciting," Marie commented. "I didn't know that newborn alpaca babies were so quick to get to their feet," she told me.

Well, neither did I. It was an unusual day. Diesel was conceived a few hours after Eagle's birth. She keeps my memories of the day alive.

Around the same time, an alpaca female boarded on Stormwind Farm gave birth to a beige Tasman son. The owner named him Triton. This cria's birth was in no way remarkable, but the little male developed into an unusually gentle youngster. Triton and Eagle formed a special bond and spent much time playing together.

Eagle's fiber was very dense. By August, it was obvious that he was uncomfortable in the heat. Plenty of alpaca breeders shear their crias. Why not try it?

"I wouldn't do it," Carol Masters advised, "moms sometimes reject their crias after the babies have been shorn."

I could not imagine Claudia rejecting Eagle. She was a totally devoted mama.

"I don't want to do this," David resisted when asked to shear Eagle. "Remember what Carol told us," he reminded me.

"Yes, I do, but what are the odds? Let's try it just this one time," I wheedled.

Shears can be very dangerous, especially on a small cria, so we opted to remove Eagle's fiber with the much safer clippers. We started at six o'clock in the evening. Eagle happened to wander into the barn and was quickly caught and restrained. Claudia was busy grazing and didn't notice or didn't care that we had temporarily absconded with her son. The clipping went smoothly. Very soon, Eagle stood back up on the barn floor, not quite sure what had happened to him.

"He looks so much smaller," I said.

"Well, you got what you wanted," my husband replied, still not happy with my decision.

"I'm not complaining," I had to have the last word.

I like the look of a shorn alpaca. Maybe the resulting sleekness reminds me of the Whippets. It is easy to evaluate conformation once most of the fiber has been removed. A full fleece can hide many faults or, in reverse, distort excellent structure. Eagle looked conformationally correct. I was pleased.

It soon became obvious that Eagle's mother did not share my pleasure. By now, Claudia noticed Eagle missing and came in search of him. One glance at the shorn, sleek-looking cria convinced Claudia that this was not her baby. Where was her fluffy, puffy looking teddy bear? She ran out of the barn again to look outside. Seconds later, she was back in the barn. Increasingly desperate, she ran to and fro searching for her "lost" child. Within a minute, Claudia was in full panic mode. Her cries became shrill with urgency.

Meantime, Eagle wanted to nurse, as much for comfort after his shearing ordeal as from true hunger. He, of course, had no problem recognizing his mother and set off in pursuit of her. His attempts at nursing—so brave and determined—were met by Claudia with spitting, kicking, and trying to outrun him. Eagle's mother was outraged over the attempts of this "strange" cria to steal her milk.

"Oh God," I thought, "what have I done?"

I managed to herd both Claudia and Eagle into a catch pen inside the barn. The forced physical closeness hopefully would help Claudia to accept her cria. No luck. I draped the shorn fiber over Eagle's back. Nope. Eagle was crying with hunger by now, but Claudia was in no mood to listen. This shorn stranger was *not* her beautiful cria, and she was not going to allow a two-legged meddler to convince her otherwise.

I flinched as a thankfully poorly aimed kick narrowly missed Eagle's little head. Three hours had passed since the ill fated shearing. By now, Eagle was seriously hungry, probably dehydrated, and very upset about his mother's rejection of him. Nothing in his world was right.

Unlike animals with only one stomach, ruminants can't go without food for long without becoming seriously ill. Alpacas are modified ruminants. They have three stomach compartments, not four, but—as with true ruminants—their digestive system needs to be continuously fueled.

Suffering from severe pangs of guilt and seriously worried, I ran back to the house, mixed goat milk powder with warm water, and filled a bottle I had purchased for an emergency. I had even bought a special nipple that was supposed to be the best on the market for alpaca crias. Before storing it away, I had washed it repeatedly to remove the strong taste and smell of new rubber. All was ready! Nothing like being prepared!

Out in the barn, Eagle wasn't interested. "I want my mama," he cried, "get that nasty thing out of my mouth."

I used every trick in the book to get him to take the bottle. If I was stubborn in trying, he was just as stubborn in rejecting my offer. I was close to tears. All our crias had been healthy, but Eagle was exceptionally vigorous and robust. Now he would be sick because of a stupid decision on my part. He could possibly die. David was sympathetic only to a point.

"You should have listened to Carol," he stated the obvious.

"Lots of people shear their crias, and nothing bad ever happens," my misdirected anger flared.

Of course, Carol had told me not to do this. Why had I not listened? With renewed energy, I undertook another determined but ultimately futile attempt to get Eagle to drink from the bottle. Claudia would not even look at him. It was hopeless. It was now midnight, and I was exhausted from the long hours of stress.

"Go to bed," David urged, "there isn't much you can do now."

Afraid that Claudia would injure Eagle in her attempts to escape from him, I released both from the catch pen. Reluctantly, I left the alpacas and returned to the house. With a heavy heart, I undressed and tried to rest. Sleep would not come. Every few minutes, I looked at the lit-up face of the alarm clock on my nightstand. Next to me, David snored peacefully. I was torn between envy and outrage over his ability to sleep while the upsetting drama played itself out in the pasture. "Men!" I thought.

At three o'clock in the morning, I could no longer stand tossing and turning in bed. Silently, I rose in the dark and dressed. Downstairs, the Whippets were sleeping and barely stirred when I passed David's office to step out on the porch. Quickly, I pulled on my farm boots and walked toward the female pasture. There was a full moon. No flashlight was needed to guide the way. The night was very quiet, the air still and clear. It was a perfect night for walking, romance, or sitting on the porch with a good friend. I prayed that it would be a perfect night for reuniting an alpaca mama and her baby.

All alpacas, including Eagle, were silently cushed outdoors, illuminated by moonlight. Nobody rose when I entered the pasture. Despite my worries, I was suddenly overcome by a sense of profound peace and stepping outside of reality.

I looked at Claudia. She rose, stretched, and stared back at me. She had a strange expression on her face. No doubt there was discomfort—even pain—from an udder that hadn't been emptied in over nine hours.

Claudia stood motionless as I stepped in front of her. I whispered, "I will bring your baby to you now. It's Eagle. Please let him nurse."

Without another word, I turned and silently scooped up the cria. Eagle was uncharacteristically quiet as I carried him toward Claudia and gently deposited him as close to her as I dared. The moon disappeared briefly behind a cloud and then reappeared, bathing the pasture and the alpacas in a soft, silvery light.

It seemed like an enchanted world. I felt a reassuring closeness with the alpacas. They sensed the tension I tried hard to repress and seemed to give silent comfort. As if they knew what was at stake, the females all remained motionless, their eyes fixed on Claudia and Eagle. Following my instincts, I wordlessly walked away. The soft pasture cushioned my steps. At the barn's entrance, I could no longer resist temptation; I had to turn around and look. My face broke into a big smile as I observed Eagle nursing. There was no mistaking his swallowing Claudia's milk. The moonlight made it easy to see. Eagle's little tail was flipped up over his back, another sign that he was receiving nourishment. Claudia still had the strange expression on her face. She seemed confused, tense, and unsure of herself.

I held my breath. "Oh please," I prayed, "don't let her walk away from Eagle now." She didn't.

The ending to Eagle's story was not a completely happy one. Claudia never denied him access to her milk again, but she remained emotionally aloof. She never again doted on her cria or cared in the least where Eagle was or what he was doing.

It's as if she were saying, "I know that this ugly foundling is not my beautiful baby. I'll nurse it because I have milk, but don't ask me to love it."

During the day, only a very astute observer would have noticed anything amiss. Eagle played, romped, nursed, and rested along with the other Stormwind crias. Night time was enough to break my heart. The most independent alpaca cria will cush next to its mama when dark falls and things go bump in the night. Even Riverman did not sleep next to his Pearl unless both of their mamas chose to cush close to each other.

After the shearing episode, I never again saw Eagle rest closely to his mama. Claudia simply wouldn't allow it. For three evenings in a row, I found him sitting away from the group, a little outcast so lonely and shunned that tears sprang to my eyes. I started to hate my beloved "bed check" ritual.

The fourth evening held a surprise. There was Eagle, his customary distance away from Claudia and the rest of the females. Cushed next to him was his friend, Triton. A very young cria does not leave its mama at night without her permission. Triton had chosen to join his lonely friend with his mama's blessings. The sight of Eagle and Triton cushed next to each other greeted me at every bed check until they were purchased by different people and went their separate ways.

Triton consoled his friend Eagle when the latter was rejected by his dam.

My last story involving both Eagle and Triton is an amusing one. I have long come to realize that alpacas recognize the sexual differences between humans. In an earlier chapter, I wrote about our alpaca boys showing off for human females. On other farms, I've seen delinquent males challenge their human female care takers but show respect for the men. I have always believed that people who argue that profound differences don't exist between the sexes live in a dream world. Like humans, alpacas often show marked differences in behavior—depending on their sex—at a very young age. I don't find this strange or remarkable in any way.

We did have one situation with Eagle and Triton that amazed me. Both were a few months old when we started construction on a new pole barn. Although it made me a little jittery due to safety concerns, we allowed the alpacas to graze in the pasture while the barn was being constructed.

We did much of the work ourselves but hired a carpenter to erect the poles and put on a roof. While the man we called the Barn Czar was in charge, David acted as a carpenter's helper and general "go-fer."

Except at shearing time and when male visitors are present, our alpacas rarely see a human male. I take care of all the farm chores. The animals only see David on special occasions. Most times, they watch him whizz by them while he's sitting on his mower.

Two men living with them in their pasture during the day was a novelty for the alpacas. After only one day, I came to recognize a rather amusing pattern. While the females walked and grazed in the lower pasture, Triton and Eagle remained with the men. The two crias cushed side by side and watched David and the carpenter work for hours. To do this, they actually had to have their backs turned to the rest of the herd. Their physical position seemed to be a conscious choice on their part. The little males watched the men intently, with enormous concentration and keen interest in all their activities. The females showed not the slightest curiosity in either the workers or the job.

Did the crias watch because they were intrigued with the presence of males in their pasture? Or was it the building activities going on that interested them?

"Maybe they were both carpenters in an earlier life," a friend of mine joked.

It certainly was all a little strange. South American pastoralists call llamas and alpacas their "speechless brothers." While living with camelids for thousands of years, what did the South American herders and breeders observe and hear that prompted them to coin this term? What will we experience if we try to communicate with our alpacas without the assumption that they are "dumb" animals and lack the ability to understand us? Will most of my readers believe, as I do, that Triton made a conscious decision to comfort his lonely friend at night? Or will they interpret his actions as something that "just happened," with no deeper meaning?

We have not shorn any more crias on Stormwind Farm.

Ingrid administers a routine inoculation to Claudia.

Chapter 7

FARM CHORES

When we started farming with alpacas in 1997, David and I both had full time jobs on "the outside." Getting farm chores done at night and on the weekends was often a difficult juggling act. It took several years for our farm's infrastructure to be completed. Major projects such as building barns and creating pastures had to be sandwiched in between our non-farming jobs and caring for the animals. Our schedule was very tough at times, but no more so than the schedules of thousands of farmers all over the country who must combine farm work with other employment.

We are both retired now, and our days have taken on a comfortable rhythm. If retired people tell you that they're busier than ever, don't believe them. Sure, my days are filled to the brim with farm activities. I am definitely never bored. It would be silly though to pretend that my life is as hectic and exhausting as it used to be.

David is a nocturnal creature who likes to sleep late and stays up way past midnight. As a retiree, he can indulge his inner clock. I am more of a morning person but don't feel the need to rise at a specific time each day. To live without a wake-up buzzer, what luxury!

Of course, there are still plenty of mornings when the alarm pulls me out of a cozy bed. I prefer to rise very early during birthing season, especially when I've observed subtle signs of pre-labor the previous day. On weekends, I often leave the farm before sunrise to attend alpaca related events. The animals must be cared for before I depart for the day.

Other than those times, I allow the sun and the birds' chirping to wake me. After decades of rushing out of the house on weekday mornings, I savor my quiet and leisurely breakfast. Truth be told, I almost resent it when, on rare occasions, David gets up early and invades my breakfast solitude. I eat whole grain bread or raw oatmeal with fruit at the kitchen table. I read or write while I drink a cup of coffee. Breakfast over, it's time to let out the Whippets. Rainy and Diesel charge out the kitchen door. Chi-Chi hates to go outside and needs gentle prompting. Once she's completed her business, she has her nose pressed against the glass of the patio door. She wants back in! Chi-Chi's odd behavioral pattern started several years ago, seemingly overnight. I don't know if she had an encounter with a wild animal that really frightened her, but she's obviously never gotten over her fear. On nice days, Rainy and Diesel stay outside for a few hours. If it's cold or raining, I wait for them to return inside before I head out to the barns and pastures to tackle farm chores.

We normally have between fifteen and twenty-five alpacas on Stormwind Farm.

Many people have asked me, "How much work is it to take care of them?"

"That's an impossible question to answer in one or two sentences," I always reply.

Then I go on to explain that the answer depends on numerous variables, not the least of which is the stamina and strength of the person asking the question.

"Have you recently cared for horses?" I usually inquire. If farm visitors nod to the positive, I smile, "Then raising alpacas will be very little work for you."

Often the answer is, "No, I've never had a farm or raised any animals."

Then I reply somewhat sternly, "Raising alpacas is a lot of work."

I personally don't consider caring for twenty alpacas a full-time job. A herd of this size should not require eight or more hours of work each day. This is especially true if the caretaker is young and strong. However, there are people of all ages who may find even a smaller herd burdensome to maintain.

In my opinion, the size of the farm itself determines much of the work load. Other variables are the number and condition of farm buildings, the farm's layout, and the organizational skills of the farmer. People who are not accustomed to physical labor will usually experience a rude awakening when they begin to work on their newly-purchased farm. Some adjust and come to love the work while others complain and sell their herd within the first year. Of course, prospective alpaca farmers should remember that there are no free weekends. The animals must be cared for seven days a week.

My daily alpaca morning chores start with feeding each animal a very small amount of a pelleted specialty feed. The pellets are spread in individual, plastic feed dishes at the rate of roughly three ounces per alpaca per day. The dishes hook over the livestock panels that divide each barn into a loafing area for the alpacas and a housekeeping or service section. In the female barn, the service section is quite large. Most of the hay supply for the year and the shearing table are stored there. The smaller male barn has a service area that holds only fifty hay bales, a small desk, a chair, and feed storage containers.

After the alpacas have consumed their pellets, I add a few flakes of hay to what's left from the previous day. If there's no threat of rain or snow, the flakes are spread on the pasture. Hay is always placed well away from any dung piles even though the latter are faithfully cleaned each day. During inclement weather, hay is kept in the barn. Hay is never rationed. The alpacas can eat their fill. Of course, they consume only tiny amounts when pasture growth is abundant.

We don't have automatic waterers. Each barn has two to three water buckets hanging in various locations. I scrub and refill them after the morning feeding. During the cold months, the alpacas drink warm water from heated buckets.

My last routine barn chore in the morning is to check the feed bins holding minerals. In my experience, females and crias consume far more minerals than the males. That makes sense. Crias are growing, and females are usually pregnant, nursing, or both. I top off the contents of the bins if necessary.

That leaves picking up dung as the last morning chore. Alpaca dung is firm in consistency and roughly the size of coffee beans. I rake the beans into small piles and scoop them into buckets. The buckets are then emptied into composting bins that I constructed from wooden pallets.

"Oh, that sounds easy," a farm visitor commented on my daily routine.

"Yes," she nodded her head approvingly, "it doesn't seem like a lot of work at all."

"Hold it," I cautioned the enthusiastic future alpaca farmer, "I've only told you about my daily, *routine* morning chores so far."

Pearl supervises the daily dung removal from Stormwind Farm's pastures.

Even on a small farm such as ours, there's always additional work to be done. This chapter doesn't include all the chores that I take care of over the course of a year. Nevertheless, it gives readers more than a glimpse of running an alpaca farm without employees. Occasionally, family or friends help with chores, but those times have been very rare.

One chore I usually enjoy very much is the daily pasture walk. Although their purpose is to look for safety hazards and evaluate pasture growth, the walks are simply good exercise in fresh air. Some days, I'll come across a dead bird or the remnants of a rabbit. Those discoveries are part of farm life and to be expected. At times, the pleasure of a pasture walk is ruined by the actions of thoughtless people. What upsets me greatly are balloons or pieces of them littering our property. They drift in a pasture from the air and are impossible to guard against. Another unpleasant chore is picking up the garbage that drivers or passengers of cars traveling past our farm toss out of their car windows. A good portion of the debris is from fast food restaurants. I wish these establishments would mount a campaign to educate their customers about the dangers that littering poses to farm animals and farmers.

I also check pastures prior to mowing. During the spring and early summer, our alpacas are hard pressed to keep up with pasture growth. Grazing animals like fresh, tender grass as well as legumes and herbal plants. Mowing is necessary if plants are not to grow tall and rank. David mows while I open and close pasture gates to help speed up the job.

David mows the pastures with a diesel powered golf course mower.

Periodically, I sweep the mats that cover the barn floors and compost the remainder of old hay. New hay is delivered to us once a year, usually in July. I carry the bales into the barn where David stacks them all the way to the ceiling. There's an art to stacking hay properly so bales won't crash down and possibly injure someone.

Compared to the hard work of stacking hay, taking care of my gardens filled with perennials as well as annual flowers is a pleasure.

"You are crazy," a friend cried out when I told her that I like to weed.

So I'm crazy! I have to admit, though, that my initial gardening plans were too ambitious. With the alpaca herd growing and my business taking off in other ways, I was no longer able to keep my flower beds in pristine condition. The soil on our farm is rich and fertile. Everything grows rapidly, including weeds. It's a blessing and a curse at the same time. There was no solution but to reduce the size of the beds to more manageable dimensions.

That included the size of my vegetable garden. It's best to be realistic. I always want gardening to be a relaxing hobby, not something that I dread doing.

In addition to the gardens, trees and bushes cannot be neglected. They must be trimmed and pruned at least bi-annually, or I'll soon be facing a jungle. The alpacas take care of pruning the forsythia bushes on their side of the fence. They do a very neat and meticulous job. The remainder is up to me. I enjoy seeing our property well taken care of. It also makes good business sense. Potential customers are easily turned off by a farm's ramshackle appearance.

The long farm lane that I was so proud of has turned out to be a big pain in the neck. Pot holes appear with maddening regularity and need to be filled.

"You'll never be done with that job. You'll work on it every year," one old timer in the township told David.

I wince every time I watch a delivery truck barrel down the lane. More potholes to fill!

One farm chore not often mentioned is the burial or other disposal of dead critters. I've had to bury several dogs and a few alpaca crias on the farm. Fortunately, the soil was always soft when this sad chore had to be performed. David refuses to get involved with this work detail. One morning, I stepped into the kitchen and found a note attached to the window of the patio door.

It read: "Ingrid, I think the dogs killed something last night. Go out the door and walk to the nearest tree. At the little tree, turn left. Walk approximately ten steps. Make a quarter turn to the right. Walk fifteen steps toward the fence. I think it's a groundhog."

It was! I don't bury small, dead critters but allow the vultures to dispose of them. That's the purpose of these large and useful birds. They are a farm's natural clean-up crew. Of course, I make sure that neither dogs nor alpacas come in contact with the decaying animals.

We have never had an adult alpaca die on Stormwind Farm. It'll happen sooner or later. Among livestock farmers, composting the dead animals with saw dust has become well accepted. It's a sensible solution and one I will try in the future. Hopefully, our geriatrics are quite a few years away from forcing me to make a decision on the subject of carcass removal.

There's a good chance that our alpacas will live to be well into their twenties. Why shouldn't they? I take very good care of them. In addition to the daily chores, the alpacas are de-wormed and inoculated at regular intervals. During the winter months, crias receive a weekly dose of vitamins in paste form. For all these procedures, females and their crias are herded into a catch pen as a group. Restraint is gentle and only involves my hands. They are not haltered, and no restraining devices are used.

In contrast, the adult males are individually herded into a small enclosure for any herd health treatments. It wouldn't be safe to restrain one male, however gently, while giving the others an opportunity to jump on its back.

Toe nails are trimmed once a month. This is a dreaded chore for many alpaca breeders. Because of my handling techniques, most of our alpacas behave well. The females are haltered and the attached lead is loosely tied to a livestock panel. Harley is so cooperative that I probably don't even need to halter him.

I use a chute to contain the other males while I trim their toenails. This useful piece of equipment must be utilized with knowledge of potential danger and extreme caution! Novice owners often don't understand that forcefully restraining alpacas in a chute will not necessarily turn them into limp dishrags. Alpacas can become so frightened and react so violently that they'll injure and even kill themselves. Safe behavior in a chute has to be carefully taught, just like any other novel experience. I rarely have help during herd health days. The techniques I practice work for me.

While having their nails trimmed and being shorn are not favorite activities for the alpacas, most of them truly enjoy a frequent shower massage during hot and humid days.

"I thought you're not supposed to hose down their entire body," a novice breeder questioned me.

Oh, nonsense! Sure, when the alpacas are in full fleece, it's important to only direct a full stream of water at the legs and the underside of their bellies. Once they are shorn, I give those that like it the full treatment. They're soaked down to the skin from their heads to their toes. Breeze is positively ecstatic over my hydrotherapy. So is old Dexter. A few don't want their entire body soaked, and I don't force them to submit to it. T-Man, our California boy, doesn't like any spraying. It has to be brutally hot before he'll come running to be cooled off. Of course, we also have barn fans to keep the alpacas comfortable.

In our climate, caring for alpacas is a lot more work during hot weather than during the winter months. With all that fiber, they don't mind the cold. Our alpacas graze year around. While cold weather suits them, they very much dislike a heavy snow fall or icy conditions that force them to remain in their barns. This year, we've had more snow than what is normal for the southern part of New Jersey. We had a few hectic days! We don't own a plow. The farmer down the road from us plows our driveway. In all other areas, snow is shoveled by hand. I clear the areas in front of the barn doors and move snow away from around the pasture gates. As long as it doesn't snow too often, it's not a chore I mind doing. This year, a farm visitor volunteered for the job. Although I admit that it was nice to get a break, I did feel guilty a few times and ventured out to help.

Because of the deep snow, the training sessions I had scheduled this February for Hunter and Pilot had to be postponed. Usually, I start serious handling and training when the crias are six to seven months old. The sessions are a pleasure to me, not a chore. I'll be writing about them in a separate chapter.

Two chores that are added to my "to do" list many mornings are either managing a breeding or a pregnancy test. There are various management styles for an alpaca breeding program. They all have their merits. On Stormwind Farm, I decided that hand-breeding was the best fit for the size of our herd and the layout of barns and pastures. During hand-breeding, each mating is scheduled and supervised. Supervision doesn't mean that I hover over the animals and watch every move. With the exception of Prince, our present males are all experienced. They certainly don't need me to meddle by micromanaging their intimate moments.

When a breeding is scheduled, I first herd the female alpaca into a catch pen that is in full view of the male pasture. I halter the female and wrap its tail with vet wrap. By the time I'm done, the males have already gathered around the "bull pen" in their pasture. They're anticipating my next move! I open the pen, and the alpaca males crowd in. Deftly, I herd out all but the individual I've chosen for the female scheduled to be bred that day. The haltered male is walked to the breeding pen where the female is waiting for it. Within seconds, the male orgles and mounts the female, forcing it to cush. Experienced females sometimes cush long before the male makes contact. In any case, once the female is settled, penetration takes place. The alpacas remain in that position until the male rises. I always hope that a single breeding will result in a pregnancy. It often does.

Sure Shot's Traveling Man (T-Man) breeds Maribel. The leads were removed as soon as the photo was taken.

"You can hardly call these intimate moments, it's more like an intimate hour," David protested years ago when he watched the first time. "If you had told me," he complained, "I would have brought a lunch and a Thermos with coffee."

David was referring to the forty minutes it took Taku to complete his breeding with Breeze. Twenty to forty minutes are a perfectly normal time frame for an alpaca breeding. That's quite a chunk of time to just be idly standing around. Once the breeding is underway, and I've unclipped the lead ropes, I busy myself with cleaning up dung piles, or I perform other small chores in or around the barn. That way, I can keep an eye on what's going on and hear when the male stops orgling. That's usually a signal that the job is finished.

With a maiden female or an inexperienced male, I'll stay close to the pen. Even then, I try to remain as unobtrusive as possible. Males that have never been used at stud often need a little time to figure things out. Human interference rarely speeds up the discovery process and may very well slow things down considerably. Patience is a true virtue for the smart alpaca breeder.

One of the most frequently asked questions from the general public about alpacas is: "Do they spit?"

I'd be disappointed if they didn't. The cheapest way to test for pregnancy status is what alpaca breeders call a "behavior test." It doesn't cost anything except a few minutes of my time. Once again, the male is haltered and brought into the breeding pen. If the female is pregnant, she'll spit at the male. I know my females very well and trust what they tell me. After a few seconds of spitting, a very unhappy stud is returned to the male pasture. Twenty-four hours after a breeding, spitting may simply mean that the female has ovulated. She's not necessarily pregnant. The behavior test must be repeated at various intervals over three months before I'm satisfied that I can look forward to a new cria in roughly a year's time.

If alpacas are raised properly and treated with respect, neither females nor males will spit at humans.

Most days, I try to have all the hard physical work I planned for the day finished by noon. By then, it's time for lunch and a rest. Waking up refreshed from a nap, I check on the alpacas again and top off water buckets if there's a need. The Whippets are fed. The rest of the afternoon and the evening are spent reading, writing, and taking care of farm paper work. I keep meticulous health care and breeding records with a simple paper and pen system. Considerable hours are devoted to marketing. I spend quite a bit of that time on managing the activities of a marketing co-op. I am one of the co-op's founding members and very proud of what we accomplish each year. I work closely with two other members who serve on the board of directors with me. Additional alpaca owners help out at most of the events sponsored by our group. Their volunteer labor is very much appreciated and never taken for granted.

Around nine o'clock in the evening, I visit the pastures and barn for a last "bed check." That visit is another favorite farm chore. It's a very quiet and peaceful time. During the birthing season, I spend many minutes observing the pregnant females for signs of early labor. During the winter months, the evening checks are especially relaxing. Sometimes, I sit on an overturned muck bucket and enjoy spending quiet time with the animals I love.

"But aren't there times when you're sick of all the work and being tied down?" people ask me frequently.

Sure, there are days when I ask myself if life wouldn't be easier if caring for a house and a small property were all I had to do. Those are fleeting moments of doubt during times of rare disappointments or stress. They never last long because I cannot imagine being truly happy living a life of leisure and little purpose.

This year, one of our visitors expressed her feelings on the subject. They mirrored my own. While I wrote the first draft of this book, Maria took care of most of the routine chores on the farm,

One day she came inside, her face red from the cold and glowing with good health.

"I have to do physical work to feel good," Maria told me. "At home, I jog or go to the gym to work out, but this is so much better."

"It is?" I smiled.

"Yes," she nodded emphatically as she removed her heavy farm boots and winter coat, "jogging makes me feel good, but it really doesn't do anything else. This is better. Here my exercise has a purpose, and I can see what I've accomplished."

There is much wisdom in her words. Like Maria, I feel cranky and oddly out of sorts when I don't perform strenuous physical labor for a few days. Maybe that's why so many people nowadays are depressed and dissatisfied with their lives. There's too much sitting and not enough walking, lifting, digging, and bending with a real purpose and the satisfaction of a job well done.

Yesterday, my morning chores were interrupted by the delivery of a skid load of lime. We received forty bags. Each bag weighed forty pounds. Unfortunately, the unusually wet conditions this year made it unwise to have the driver deliver the bags all the way to the barn. The young man who delivered the skid stood on the back of the truck and handed off each bag to me. I carried the bags a few feet and stacked the entire shipment of 1,600 pounds on the ground of the parking area closest to the female barn. After I had finished my morning chores, David helped me transport the bags to the barn in a small wagon, 160 pounds at a time. Once there, we stacked them on a pallet. When we were done, David—who very much dislikes physical work even though he's done plenty in his life—stretched and said, "That felt good!"

On any alpaca farm, shearing is an annual and exhausting chore. Since the fiber harvest is at the core of what raising alpacas is all about, I've devoted a separate chapter to shearing. It's the time of the year when the reluctant farmer, David, shines and basks in my praise.

Farm chores don't leave me anywhere near as tired as the work I did as a much younger teacher. It's not that I still have energy to go dancing at night, but I never experience the absolutely mind-numbing exhaustion and bone-tired weariness I so often felt at the end of a teaching day.

This past summer, I talked to an old man who stopped at the farm after seeing our farm sign on the road. His family's roots are in Portugal, and farming is in his blood. He told me about his chickens and how he'd like to have goats.

"None of my children and grandchildren want to farm," he sighed sadly, adding, "I don't know why not. It's the best kind of life if you know how to do it."

I showed him around our place.

"Your animals look healthy," he said, a little wistfully. Then he got back in his car and waved to me as he departed.

By that time, afternoon chores were waiting. A pressing morning errand had made it necessary to postpone a pregnancy behavior test. The female I planned to test had just conveniently stepped into the barn. I closed off access to the pasture, herded Claudia into the breeding pen, and put a halter on her head. On the other side of the fence, the boys had observed the preparations and lurked in anticipation of a tryst. If everything had gone well eight days ago, T-Man would only receive a gob of spit in his face for all his troubles. I knew it would not deter him from trying his luck during future tests. It never does. That's as it should be. After all, that's one of the farm chores the alpaca males are expected to perform. They're hard workers, those alpaca boys of mine.

Spacious pastures help keep the peace among the female alpacas on Stormwind Farm.

Chapter 8

ALPACA SOAP OPERAS

When David was a boy and started to show interest in girls, his father explained to him that women are complicated creatures with complex feelings and difficult-to-understand personalities. In contrast, my father-in-law philosophized, men are straight forward and have simple needs.

"Give a man a football game on television, a beer, and a good piece of salami, and he's happy," Mr. Wood explained to his attentive son.

The salami was important. Mr. Wood liked to eat fat, including spoonfuls of mayonnaise right out of the jar.

I wonder what my late father-in-law—college educated and with a degree in aeronautical engineering—would have thought of the differences between alpaca males and females. Most likely, he'd have put a television in the male barn during football season.

It's true, the alpaca males have simple needs and desires. They eat, visit the dung pile, wrestle, and sleep. Their number one priority, however, is to breed as many females as possible.

As long as there's no open female to fight over, our males are buddies. Sure, they have their social hierarchy, but it's well established and without subtle nuances. In their case, it's not beer and salami, but pasture and hay that represent great living. It's easy to keep them happy.

In contrast, alpaca females are often embroiled in complicated social interactions. Mr. Wood was right!

"It's a soap opera out there," I always tell visitors to Stormwind Farm.

Tempers flare over real and perceived insults. Feelings are easily hurt. Friendships are formed and break up again weeks later for reasons that are not always clear to me. I've witnessed temperamental outbursts as well as quiet sulking. There are also heartwarming incidents of herd members supporting one another.

As much as the female alpacas squabble at times, they form a cohesive group. Throughout the day, they graze and rest as a unit. I rarely see one of the females off on her own, a far distance apart from her friends and other herd members. Almost all disagreements occur in the barn during prolonged inclement weather. In contrast, grazing keeps the alpacas too busy to fret over the herd's rank order.

The females' social status is always in flux. The crias are normally on the bottom of the hierarchy. They're expected to defer to all adults. To complicate matters, their status within the herd is largely determined by their mother's status. A young adult daughter of a low-ranking female may therefore be afraid to challenge the cria of a high status mother. Low-level, older females can sometimes elevate their status by befriending the cria of a higher ranking mama. Years ago, a boarded female on our farm accomplished this social feat by making friends with Breeze's daughter, Verona. Yes, the interactions between adult females and all the crias living within a herd are complex.

Most adults are intensely curious about any newborn and often lavish quite a bit of attention on another mama's offspring immediately following the birth. The crias are also watched over by the entire herd as they're growing up. That said, most females nursing a cria will not permit a herd mate's baby to closely approach them. Quite wisely, the mamas protect their milk supply for the benefit of their own infants. Nevertheless, adults are usually fairly patient with the female crias that belong to other mothers.

Male crias, especially the fresh and bold ones, are often sharply disciplined. If a male is the only cria in a herd, the females may be more willing to indulge it. This was true when Nicholas was the lone alpaca baby on Stormwind Farm for a short period of time. Nicholas had several other things going in his favor. His mother was Breeze, the highest ranking female in the herd. He was also well-behaved. There were hardly ever any tell-tale gobs of green spit on his face or on his neck. When Christina, a young college student, came to take photographs of our alpacas, she was very observant.

"The adults are all so protective of Nicholas," Christina marveled at how the females all cared about the cria's safety.

Outside of the main herd dynamics, the crias have their own playground hierarchy. Contrary to what people may think, the physically largest or oldest cria is not necessarily the boss. Last year, we purchased back two females, Bella and Apple, which had been bred, born, and raised on Stormwind Farm. Bella's cria, the pint-sized Betsy, arrived along with the adults.

"Betsy was the cria boss on our farm," her breeder, my friend Jerry, told me.

I laughed. Tiny Betsy didn't exactly fit the bill of a bold ruler. I should have known better. Betsy is Breeze's granddaughter. Ha! Interestingly, Betsy's mother, Bella, is sweet and pretty much keeps to herself. If challenged by another female, she usually backs down and walks away to diffuse the situation. In contrast, Apple's daughter, Cider, has the same self-assurance as Betsy did. Her body language is clear in its message to the other crias: "I'm nice, but I'm tough. Don't mess with me."

The social status of the adult female alpacas seems largely to be dependent on pregnancies and nursing a cria. Fertility is the ultimate status symbol! At the top of the hierarchy are the females that are pregnant and nursing a cria at the same time. Next are the pregnant females without a cria at side. It may be their first pregnancy or, for whatever reason, I chose to skip a season and did not rebreed them several weeks after giving birth. At Stormwind Farm, we normally rebreed nineteen to thirty days after birth. Women flinch when they hear this; it is a normal time frame for healthy camelids.

Breeze is the rare exception to the herd's hierarchy rules. This past winter, Breeze had baby Nicholas at side but was not pregnant. I didn't want to risk a late winter birth for her next cria and kept her open, which means unbred in alpaca breeder lingo. Breeze's empty womb did not diminish her status. She remained firmly enthroned as the queen of the herd.

Newcomers to the farm's herd may initially dwell at the bottom of the social structure despite being pregnant and nursing a baby. Their immediate status upon entry to the herd depends very much on their level of confidence and personality.

On the lowest rung of the power ladder perch the females that aborted their crias or whose babies died during or shortly after birth. Early abortions or reabsorption of a fetus are fairly common with alpacas. Twins are rarely carried to term. It's heartbreaking when a female carries a pregnancy to full term, but the cria is born dead. It happens on all farms sooner or later.

Claudia's story is a good example of loss of status due to a dead cria. It took Claudia several years to rise to one of the top positions in the herd. She earned the spot by getting pregnant and delivering babies like clockwork. How did I know that Claudia had successfully reached her goal? Fan space! During the summer months, I run three fans in the female barn. The circulating air makes the entire barn more comfortable, but the choice seats are right in front of the fans themselves. About two years ago, Claudia garnered one of these coveted seats. Last year, I suspected something was wrong with her pregnancy when I found Claudia cushed in the back of the barn. It wasn't scorchingly hot, but I knew that she would not abandon her fan privilege without good reason. The next day, she delivered a fully-formed but dead cria with assistance from our veterinarian. It was Claudia's first unsuccessful pregnancy. After a month of rest, I rebred her. Three days after the breeding, I walked into the barn at noon and smiled broadly. Claudia was cushed in front of the fan. A pregnancy behavior test confirmed what I already knew. Claudia was pregnant again!

When she was younger, Claudia tried very hard to take over Breeze's role as the herd's leader. She gave up her ambitious scheming when it became obvious that not one of the other females was willing to support her quest.

Sanibel, a more recent newcomer to the Stormwind herd, also launched a serious campaign to oust the old herd boss. A prolonged spitting war finally left Breeze firmly in control. When Sanibel realized the utter futility of her attempts, she pouted. Big time! I actually became somewhat concerned when she stayed away from the other alpacas for several days. Eventually, Sanibel ended her self-imposed isolation and once again mingled with the herd. I guess the role of suffering victim became too boring after a while. The birth of her handsome son, Hunter, did a lot to restore Sanibel's confidence. She turned out to be a great mama.

Sanibel's half sister, Maribel, is a big, beautiful female. So far, she's displayed the proper deferential behavior of a maiden alpaca toward her elders. It'll be interesting to see what will happen once she is pregnant.

Maribel acts deferential toward her elders.

Another young female, Caramel, came to us at the age of six months. Since we had not purchased her mother, Caramel arrived alone—a tiny cria with eye-catching conformation and very soft, crimpy fiber. I adored her from the very beginning.

"She is just so cool," I told my friend, Kate, on whose farm Caramel had been boarded, "she fits in so well, you'd never know she wasn't born and raised here."

Caramel calmly accepted the initially unfriendly reactions from the established herd members. She took mental notes of herd hierarchy rules and adjusted her behavior accordingly.

For example, Caramel immediately registered the fact that Breeze gets highly irate if anyone approaches her while her cria is nursing. She nimbly avoided Breeze's vicinity after the old herd boss disciplined her for invading her private space. What I liked was the fact that Caramel did not seem upset by the discipline but simply filed the knowledge away for future reference.

Occasionally, females that are sent to Stormwind Farm to be bred to our males join our herd. Because of barn space, pasture growth, and biosecurity, I prefer to keep such visitors to a minimum. Additionally, a female with a strong personality can cause major social upsets. Repeat visitors—of which we've had a few—are nice to have because social boundaries are clear right from the minute they step into our pasture. Alpacas have long memories.

Some individuals stake a personal claim to a particular section of barn space and defend it against all comers. There are others that are willing to settle where there is room without fussing.

"Just give me a dry, comfortable spot anywhere in the barn," Bella requests companionably.

None wish to rest while touching another alpaca. Alpaca females like to live with companions, but they definitely don't want to be crowded. Our Whippets always snuggle closely to one another. In contrast, each alpaca prefers its private space. Adults exempt only their crias from this social rule.

Like all prey animals, alpacas are very aware of any changes in their environment. Since they trust me, most are not interested when I handle or train their herd mates.

"Oh, you're cutting Breeze's toenails? I'll keep my distance and graze." Sanibel, along with most of the other Stormwind alpacas, minds her own business and leaves the area near the catch pen.

The rest of the herd follows. Of course, there is always one individual that feels the need to keep track of the smallest activity on the farm.

"Toenails? Let me check what you're doing. Last I remember, you cut one of Harley's too far into the quick, and it bled. You need supervision!" With that, busybody Pearl sticks her neck through the catch pen.

Harley is aggravated. He doesn't mind me cutting his nails in the least, but he doesn't want Pearl touching him while I'm snipping away with a pair of pruning shears.

By the time I've trimmed the first nail, Libby has already reached the other end of the pasture. I am convinced that the quiet Libby is often annoyed by Pearl. The latter is flamboyant and craves attention. Although the two females have spent almost their entire lives together, they are not close at all. Most days, the two alpacas barely acknowledge each other's presence.

Just like human females, alpacas vary in their preferences of a partner. "One of my females absolutely refuses to cush for the new male we bought. I'm ready to tear my hair out," a fellow breeder reported.

I understood his frustration. He had paid a huge sum of money for a male with several show championships to its name and was eager to have his investment pay off. If a sexually experienced female on our farm violently rejected a new partner, I would accept the message and refrain from forcing the alpaca to mate with this male. Like all living creatures, camelids are not machines that can be programmed to function in a certain way.

Experiments with mice show that female mice are capable of identifying males that are genetically similar to them. Given a choice, the mice used in the research selected partners that differed genetically from them, especially in the genes involving the immune system.

Sometimes, an experienced, open female will lose patience with a young male that is shy about mounting it or doesn't orgle. It's not so rare for females to reject an unschooled male. There are few Demi Moores or Madonnas in the alpaca world. Most alpaca females are not interested in youthful boy toys but prefer their men to have experience and social standing in their community. All females watch very intently when two males fight with each other. While the males are chest butting, wrestling, and screaming, you could hear a pin drop in the female pasture. That doesn't mean that all alpaca females prefer a noisy hoodlum over the quiet cowboy type.

On our farm, males and females can interact to some extent because their pastures share a fence line. I make breeding decisions based on variables such as size, conformation, fiber quality, color, and several others. If I notice, however, that an alpaca female shows interest in one male to the total exclusion of all others, I pay attention and abide by its wishes. The way I figure it, the animal knows something that the study of pedigrees did not reveal to me.

It's always interesting to observe individual alpacas during the mating act, especially the reaction of the females. Some act totally indifferent and even eat grass or chew cud while being bred. Others are initially eager but quickly grow impatient. If the breeding lasts beyond ten minutes, Claudia, for example, gets up and throws off the male. She's a big girl and gets to decide when the fun is over. Miraculously, she's always pregnant after those ten minutes. She never seems to care about her partner's identity and rarely interacts with the males at the fence line. That's not true of other females in the herd. Libby, for example, showed a distinct preference for Tasman long before she was bred to him.

Then there are times when I feel that a female expresses true passion for a particular male. When bred to Tasman, Caramel turned her head toward him and nuzzled him as soon as he made contact with her. Tasman reciprocated, and they nuzzled and smooched during the entire breeding time. The lovers continued to show interest in each other long after Tasman had completed the time consuming, drawn out ejaculation process that is normal for an alpaca male.

In contrast to Caramel, the eaters and cud chewers often deliver a swift kick to the male's chest once the sexual act has reached its conclusion. The "sperm donor" is rudely reminded that it accomplished what it came for, and further dalliances are not desired.

The male that received the most loving and universal attention from our females was a fawn male named Taku. We owned him for several years. He was a gentle fellow and actually loved it when I scratched his back. Despite my attention, he always treated me like a gentleman. There was never even a hint of Taku challenging my authority. Although he appeared mild mannered, Taku was unmistakably the boss in the male pastures. The other males acknowledged his high status. Tasman only took over the top job once Taku had left the farm. Taku was naturally chunky but without showing flabby fat. The alpaca girls found him irresistibly sexy. Even the pregnant ones kissed him through the wire mesh fence.

His arrival on our farm was connected with a frightening experience that was more cop show than soap opera. In those days, I was still teaching in an elementary school within a twenty minute drive from the farm. Contrary to public perceptions, most teachers work well beyond their contracted hours. Many, like I did, take paperwork home at night instead of staying in the school building past dismissal time to grade papers or prepare lessons. I was always willing, however, to accommodate working parents, often meeting them early in the morning or after normal school hours.

The delivery of Taku was scheduled for 5:00 P.M. on a Tuesday. Prior to making the arrangements for his arrival, I had already scheduled a parent conference at 3:30 P.M. on that particular day. After contemplating the potential conflicts in my schedule, I decided that a full hour would be sufficient to discuss all concerns that the parents and I had about the child and still get home in plenty of time to see the trailer pulling into our long farm lane. The day before the scheduled delivery of our new alpaca male, the seller called.

"I'm very sorry," she said, "but I can't accommodate your schedule. I'll have to arrive around 4:00 P.M. or possibly earlier."

Reluctantly, I rescheduled the parent conference for another day. Taku arrived at the pre-arranged hour, and I was thrilled to have this beautiful alpaca join our herd.

The next morning, I found out what had happened in school after I left at our regular dismissal time. A young woman who taught in a classroom down the hall from me had stayed to work and told me the details. Around 4:00 P.M., a teenager peppered the back of the school building with a spray of bullets. My colleague had the presence of mind to drop to the floor when the shooting started. She crawled out of the room on her hands and knees all the way to the front office, closely hugging the walls furthest away from the juvenile gun man. One bullet pierced a window in the room where I had scheduled the conference. The parents and I could have easily been sitting or standing in its path had it not been for the delivery of Taku.

I was deeply shaken. "You know, I don't even care if Taku sires a single cria," I told my astonished husband, "he may very well have saved my life."

Luckily, Taku experienced no difficulties in the fertility department. Not only did he produce quite a few nice crias for us, he also made many alpaca females very happy. They sure loved his chunky body. Taku was a hunk and had male charisma as far as our females were concerned.

While some females have a definite preference for a specific male, the Stormwind alpaca males remember which females they bred in a given year. This may sound utterly crazy to some people yet I am convinced that it is true. The males' behavior in the bull pen clearly shows that they remember. They rarely challenge the right of the male that performed the original breeding to behavior test the female and possibly get another opportunity to mate. Upon further thought, this should not surprise us. An excellent memory is one of the protective skills of prey animals. They remember where predators lurk or which plants made them sick when they grazed them. Why wouldn't a male remember the female it mated with a month or even a year ago?

There is absolutely no doubt in my mind that alpacas recognize one another as individuals. People who do not believe me need to talk to the owner of a farm where two males—both of whom get along well with other pasture mates—hate each other so much that they seriously try to kill each other unless they are separated. I know of several such cases. Luckily, we've never had that problem. Most of the time, life is pretty peaceful in our pastures.

The alpacas of Stormwind Farm are a community, with the joys, sadness, squabbles, and power plays all creatures experience when they live or work within a group. There are the bold, the shy, the confident, and the worriers. There are those that enjoy and promote palace intrigues, while others plead, "Please, just leave me alone so I can raise my babies in peace."

"My Goodness, you talk about them like they're people," a visitor to Stormwind Farm cried out. Her tone of voice did not register approval.

"I know very well that my alpacas are not people dressed up in fleeces," I defended my position. "As a matter of fact," I continued, "one of the reasons the alpacas on our farm are so comfortable around humans is precisely because I do not treat them like they are human themselves."

"What do you mean?" the woman asked, more than a little confused now.

"The soap operas are strictly an alpaca production while I am a quiet observer," I explained, adding, "just because the alpacas are not human doesn't mean that we can't acknowledge each alpaca's unique personality traits and the herd members' social interactions."

The Stormwind Farm alpaca soap operas are sometimes full of drama, but no harm is done. If anything, they are amusing even though they are far more than entertainment for me, the alpaca caretaker. Observing the social interactions and dramas unfold in the barns and on the pastures helps me to understand the animals.

Among other things, I've learned to recognize the alpacas' fears as well as what makes them feel safe and comfortable. Dr. Temple Grandin—the animal scientist who advocates for more humane handling techniques of livestock in slaughter facilities—is convinced that fear is far worse for animals to endure than pain. In my opinion, that's certainly true for alpacas. I can't remove all stimuli and procedures that produce fear in our animals, but I can reduce them to a bare minimum. However, it is neither my place nor my desire to intervene in the alpacas' daily interactions with one another. I do not try to change or manipulate the herd hierarchy to my liking.

Over the years, the alpacas taught me the language that's unique to their species. I try to communicate with them in ways that show my respect for their "otherness." Yes, my visitor had it all wrong. People who anthropomorphize alpacas actually show disrespect for them.

Their message is: "These animals are only desirable and have value if they act human. It is not possible to like and respect them as alpacas."

I don't feel that way at all. We shouldn't need to "humanize" other species to enjoy their presence in our lives. Alpacas are neither human nor are they fiber machines without emotions. The truth does not lie in either extreme.

They act, think, and feel as alpacas and, as my fellow breeder and friend, Alice Brown, always says, "They're good at it!"

Are my interpretations of our alpacas' behavior fanciful flights of imagination? I don't believe so. I don't claim to understand all the delicate nuances of alpaca behavior. The South American herders, who virtually live with their animals around the clock, probably understand alpacas on a much deeper level than I ever will. Regardless, I strive daily to improve my level of communication with the animals I call my pasture companions.

Come to think of it, it's not strictly true that I am only a quiet observer in the alpaca soap operas played out on Stormwind Farm. I act in them as well, but mostly in a supporting role. That's as it should be.

Sunflowers in full bloom attract bees and birds to Stormwind Farm.

Chapter 9

Rabbits, Rodents, and Other Critters

Almost any farm is home to wild animals. Although small by farming standards, Stormwind Farm is no exception. In addition to the permanent wild residents, there are the seasonal visitors. Some critters only appear occasionally or just a single time, never to be seen again. Most prominently visible are what a friend calls "the other alpacas." Of course, deer are not in the camelid family, but—like the alpacas—they are both ruminants as well as prey animals. The color of deer changes with the seasons. At times, it is identical to that of a fawn-colored male we had at the farm for several years. Quite often, I'd do a double take, afraid that Taku had somehow escaped from the fenced pasture and was roaming in the buffer zone between pasture and protected wetlands in the back of our farm.

The wetlands area is a tiny wildlife sanctuary. It is not entered by humans. Throughout the year, deer freely leave their hiding places in the wetlands and browse in the buffer zone. The alpacas have learned to ignore them. The wild ruminants never come within touching distance of the domesticated animals that vaguely resemble them, especially after the alpacas have been shorn. I have never seen deer inside one of the pastures or discovered evidence of such activity. Our fences are five feet high. Alpaca farmers with lower fences often see deer jump in and out of their pastures. My friend, Kate, once found a tiny fawn caught inside the fence line of her Pennsylvania farm. It screamed at the top of its lungs as Kate carried it out of the pasture gate.

In the early days, we used to see many groundhogs. They waddled boldly up to the fence enclosing the Whippet yard, stood on their hind legs, and hissed aggressively. The Whippets, with Rainy leading the charge in her younger days, killed quite a few of the furry invaders if the groundhogs managed to get inside canine territory. I was not happy about this. A groundhog can severely injure an attacking dog by slashing it with its teeth. Some of the specimen we saw looked as heavy or heavier than one of our dogs. The weight of a Whippet can range from twenty to forty pounds.

The huge holes dug by groundhogs are a constant danger to farmers who plow the ground or harvest a field of hay. They're a safety hazard on our small farm as well. Nevertheless, neither David nor I are keen on the thought of our dogs tearing wild animals apart.

Although the dogs are confined to their play area, we cannot prevent wild critters from entering it. At night, we turn on outdoor lights and knock on the door. This alerts any wildlife that the dogs are about to rush out of the house. It's not always enough to prevent a successful hunt. Whippets are much, much faster than the average dog. The most likely victim falling prey to our dogs is one of the numerous rabbits that populate the farm. The slow, the foolish, and the not-so-bright are killed by either the Whippets or the feral cats that prowl the perimeter of the pastures and dog yard. The smart and savvy rabbits live underneath the wooden hay pallets in the alpaca barn. Their peace is disturbed only once a year when I pick up the pallets to clean the area before our yearly hay delivery. Although alpacas and barn rabbits live in the same dwelling, they rarely encounter one another indoors.

Grey squirrels are numerous in our county. Our farm is surrounded by trees, but I've seen only one squirrel in the years we've lived here. It frolicked energetically next to the kennel. That day, Diesel came in the house sporting a large, bloody scratch on her nose. I never saw the squirrel again. The same goes for a single chipmunk. I found it dead, its bloated body floating in a water bucket inside the boy barn.

"This is horrible," a friend of mine cried when she previewed this chapter, "it's all about killing and being killed."

She lives in the suburbs and feeds the squirrels. Well, yes, life on a farm does not just include adorable tableaux of Bambi and Thumper. Unfortunately, farm reality is often more about smelly skunks and raccoons with rabies. We haven't encountered either species on our farm. I am not complaining! I rather have my hands full controlling the mice and rats that can only be kept at bay with a strictly timed elimination program.

Rodents are the least desirable furry animals on just about any farm. I am meticulous about keeping barns and pastures clean, but field mice are part of farm life. You can't raise livestock without maintaining a manure pile somewhere on the property. Unfortunately, rats are attracted by dung. We use poison to kill rodents. I'd prefer a barn cat or two but have rejected any offers so far. With the Whippets around, the cats wouldn't last long. Our rodent control choices are therefore limited.

Due to a childhood experience, I am squeamish about rodents. I have very distinct memories of many things that happened when I was very little, a few going back to my toddler years. My family in Germany had vineyards and sold wine on a small commercial scale. The temperature in the wine cellars was always cool. Occasionally, perishable groceries were kept there. This was in 1952, long before the average German family owned a refrigerator. I was two years old when I accompanied a great-aunt I called Goodi to the cellar to fetch a pound of butter. As soon as Goodi opened the heavy cellar door, I saw a furry, little creature scurry past us. I was delighted with what I thought was the discovery of a puppy in the dark cellar. Happy and excited, I called out the good news and pointed to the "puppy." My great-aunt's blood curdling screams, our hasty exit, and the loud slamming of the cellar door confused me to no end. Her frightened cries of "It's a rat, it's a rat" were even more of a puzzle. Obviously, the little creature hadn't been a puppy, but it was cute and not scary at all. Why all the screaming?

A few minutes later, my uncle Vitus's laughter confirmed once and for all to my two-year-old's mind that adults were sometimes just too complicated to figure out. Although I felt no fear at the time, Goodi's outburst nevertheless must have left a lasting impression on me. I now shudder at the sight of a rat and could not even bring myself to pick up the harmless pet rats my son and a former girlfriend kept in their apartment.

To this day, I vividly remember my total confusion over Goodi's hysterical reaction and my uncle's amused response to the drama. Neither made sense to me at the time. This is how animals must often feel when they can't figure out human motives and reactions to what they consider perfectly normal and reasonable behavior.

Regardless of my own distaste for rodents, I'll never understand the blank hatred that some people feel toward certain animals or insects. It's a hatred fueled by fear and often ignorance of the important role the animal or insect plays in our environment.

Spiders and bats often produce strong feelings of antipathy in people. Spider webs are natural fly traps. If at all possible, I will leave them undisturbed in the barn during fly season. Bats are one of the most beneficial species to have on a livestock farm. They consume large numbers of mosquitoes and other insects. Our neighbors installed nesting boxes for bats on their place. Presently, the East Coast bat population is suffering from a fungal infection that's killing bats in huge numbers. Environmentalists are already worried about the fallout.

We should be equally concerned about a problem that worries many bee keepers. All over the United States, producers are battling mite infestations of their hives. It's no wonder! There are just too many harmful chemicals in our environment. The average person can't tell a bee from a wasp and has no clue how the lack of pollinating insects is already affecting our food supply. On Stormwind Farm, I've planted perennials that encourage the presence of honey bees and bumble bees.

Our farm is also home to a species of wasps that are fly predators. These wasps build mud nests in trees and barn crevices and are harmless if left undisturbed. Another beneficial insect species is the dung fly. To the untrained eye, they resemble wasps. They have absolutely no interest in humans or animals and do not sting. They are way too busy buzzing around dung piles. The larvae that hatch from their eggs speed decomposition of manure. This helps to control the common flies that bother animals and people. I am thrilled to see the dung fly population increase with each year that we keep alpacas on Stormwind Farm.

The butterfly bush growing just beyond the dining room window attracts—as promised in gardening literature—lots of colorful butterflies as well as tiny hummingbirds.

Even without conventional bird feeders, we have many different kind of wild birds on Stormwind Farm. Unfortunately, I know very little about birds and cannot identify all the species that make their home here. I did recognize the killdeer that built their nests on our farm in the early years. They are interesting birds because they pretend to be lame to lure predators away from their young. Flocks of golden finches feed on the seeds my large sunflowers produce each year. Red cardinals, robins, and blue birds make their homes on our farm. In both barns, sparrows are plentiful.

Initially, I welcomed the little birds nesting in the barns. Their cheerful twittering and chirping seemed part of a healthy barn environment. Eventually, though, their numbers increased to the point of being a nuisance. Four shiny pie plates, one hanging in front of each barn entrance, helped to keep the feathered barn population under control for a while. I later added a fake owl. The birds were not fooled for long.

One bird species I'd like to encourage are purple martins. Each bird consumes huge amounts of mosquitoes during the summer months. Purple martins enjoy living in close contact with humans. The environment has to be just right to attract them. Their houses cannot be too close to a building or a tree. My friends, Ralph and Connie, have a purple martin colony on their alpaca farm near the New Jersey shore. They have virtually no mosquitoes or flies on their property. Each spring, an early "scout" arrives to check out the nesting boxes Ralph provides for them. Purple martins spend their winters in South America.

Another useful, semi-domesticated bird is the Guinea hen. Many farmers in New Jersey keep Guinea hens because a small flock makes short shrift of the ticks that reproduce in vast numbers in New Jersey's hot, humid climate. Of course, Guinea hens can fly and don't always hang around. They like to roost in trees and provide a farm with a natural alarm system against strangers.

Domesticated chickens are more easily contained. My paternal grandparents' chickens and bees were my first childhood introduction to useful farm animals and insects. David wants nothing to do with either species. I have to be content to visit friends with beehives and chicken coops. Each morning, I hear our neighbor's roosters crow. I love the sound and find it oddly comforting.

We may not have chickens, but chicken hawks and vultures glide daily over the farm looking for prey. I never left tiny puppies outside without their dam to defend them as well as the overturned top of a plastic travel crate to serve as their shelter. I'm not sure I would ever risk sending a Chihuahua or another one of the miniature pocket pooches into our dog yard or a pasture without human supervision.

Quite often, when an alpaca cria is born, I observe vultures circling overhead or boldly perching on a fence post. Vultures and crows have been known to pick the eyes out of newborn lambs. It's a thought too horrible to contemplate, but nature is often cruel.

A couple of Canada geese visit each year. Luckily, the Canadian lovers remain childless or perhaps hide their goslings on another farm. In New

Jersey and probably other surrounding states, parks and school grounds are often covered with goose droppings. When I say covered, I mean that literally. Goose droppings are found in every square foot. We would not be able to raise alpacas under such conditions. I do enjoy the sight and sounds of flocks of geese flying over the farm in their famous V-formation. It's also hard not to like a bird that stays faithful to its partner for life.

A few times, wild turkeys wandered around the mowed strip of grass encircling our pastures. Although wild turkeys are abundant in other areas of New Jersey, their sightings on our farm have been rare.

Because of the wetlands and a nearby stream, I assume that we have plenty of snakes living in the farm's vicinity. They must be very secretive creatures since I've seen only three in the more than fifteen years we've lived here. One snake was the size of my little finger. Diesel caught and killed a much larger one in the dog yard. I found the third and longest snake coiled tightly underneath an overturned bucket. Upon discovery, it quickly slithered away. Since snakes keep down a rodent population, I don't mind having them around. Many people have an almost irrational fear of snakes. Livestock farmers should welcome those that are not poisonous and completely harmless to people, farm animals, and pets.

In addition to snakes, there are probably lots of turtles living in the wetlands and along Barker's Brook, a small stream that runs close to our land. We occasionally see a turtle lumbering across one of the township's back roads. On the farm, I've only encountered two. One was smaller than my hand and appeared on our back patio seemingly out of nowhere. The other one was huge. During a rainy spring, it crawled out of a muddy area in the middle of our largest pasture and looked positively formidable.

Foxes are still fairly abundant in our area. One time, I watched a fox run up our lane in broad daylight. That alone would hardly have been occasion for great excitement. As luck would have it, I was in the middle of supervising a breeding between our Whippet bitch Stormy and a visiting stud dog. Bruiser came from Georgia and had been delivered to Stormwind Farm with the help of a travel relay organized by friends. He had been a great racing dog in his prime and was a mellow and loving companion. I feared that, due to his advanced age, he would no longer be fertile. Unfortunately, that turned out to be the case. Multiple breedings did not result in puppies, but one of them left me with an unusual memory.

The first breeding took place on our front porch. With much experience under his belt, Bruiser achieved penetration and a tie in mere seconds. As is custom, I gently turned the male around. He now faced the house door while Stormy faced the lane in the opposite direction. Both dogs were firmly attached to each other when the fox—looking neither right nor left—trotted steadily closer towards the scene of the breeding.

Bruiser of course did not see him and was in any case preoccupied with physical urges and pleasures. Stormy took notice. Whippets are sighthounds. Compared to breeds of other canine groups, the aptly named sighthounds have excellent vision. Stormy's ears went up, and her body tensed as if to spring forward and give chase.

"Oh no," I fretted, "she'll pull poor Bruiser to pieces."

Quickly, I tightened the martingale collar around Stormy's neck and placed a firm hand across her shoulder blades. The fox passed the house on its way to the forest, and things went back to normal, or what passes for normal on Stormwind Farm.

I planned to give the litter a fox theme, such as Foxfire, Foxy Lady, etc., but with no puppies to show for Bruiser's labor, those plans came to naught.

To the great surprise of people living in New Jersey's cities and suburbs, the state has a fairly large coyote population. When we first moved to Stormwind Farm, I observed a coyote trot leisurely past the rear pasture fence carrying a huge rabbit in its mouth. Around the same time, my friend Barbara watched one sauntering past her chicken house. Barbara lived in the same township then, but across a major highway. I have neither seen nor heard another coyote since then. An hour's driving time south, my friend, Ralph, listens to coyotes yipping around his farm most nights. He added strands of electrified wire to his pasture fences.

Coyotes are highly adaptable to almost any environment. On a farm, they can be immensely helpful in keeping the rodent population under control. Unfortunately, coyotes as well as bears, mountain lions, and wolves cause great losses to livestock farmers and ranchers in the United States. Increasingly, livestock producers who seek to protect their pastured animals come under attack from environmental extremists. That's unfortunate.

Livestock species contribute to the genetic diversity of our planet. They provide a huge variety of products for human consumption. Food and fiber products are only the beginning of their usefulness to humans. For example, scientists at the Laboratory of Genomic Diversity (National Cancer Institute) in Frederick, Maryland mapped the alpaca genome. While the knowledge gleaned from the research helps alpaca breeders, it is also used to help humans who are suffering from cancer.

Most livestock farmers do not wish to eradicate all predatory species from the planet, nor do they hope to totally displace wild prey species competing with their livestock for grazing land. Good livestock farmers are very much aware of the fragile state of the environment they live in, much more so than the folks residing in cities or suburbs who fund the non-profit organizations that agitate for the obliteration of all domesticated livestock in this country.

Graziers feel passionate about being good stewards of the land. You can't be a grazier and not be concerned and knowledgeable about soil fertility, biodiversity, and the impact of the complex interaction of all species on grazing land.

All that most livestock farmers and ranchers ask from the public is some common sense and a willingness to compromise when predator and other wildlife issues conflict with a livestock operation. On remote ranches, livestock losses due to predators can be devastating.

There is a renewed interest in learning about farm life among city dwellers. Unfortunately, there is also an alarming disconnect from the realities of farming. For example, a very nice man came to Stormwind Farm a few weeks ago.

After introducing himself, he politely asked, "May I have some of your animal excretions?" I knew exactly what he was talking about when he added, "I brought a bucket."

Of course, I gave him the dung he wanted for his garden.

I think that farmers have not done enough to educate the general public. In past generations, they didn't have to take precious time away from their farm work to become teachers in the truest sense of the word. With only a tiny segment of the US population involved in farming, education has become a necessity.

How would adults—living all their lives in a city—know that a large deer population will make crop farming impossible? Do they realize that these crops include the corn eaten at their picnics and the apples they enjoy in their pies? Would the same people know enough to tell a happy birthday girl that her balloons drifting off to faraway places will possibly cause the agonizing death of a cow or a goat—or perhaps the alpaca whose fiber was used for the winter hat the child received as a gift? Do the suburban parents who moved to the country explain to their teenage son that the ATV he drove through a neighbor's soybean field not only destroyed crops but caused severe soil compaction? Without education, the term soil compaction is not likely to be part of their vocabulary.

The public needs to realize that farming is not a hobby but has to generate profits for those performing the labor and investing in their farm's infrastructure. Farmers have to speak up and firmly tell people, "If you want us and what we offer, you can't make it impossible for us to make a living."

If hunting is banned and an exploding wildlife population consumes crops and kills livestock, farmers and ranchers will stop planting crops and raising livestock. The end result is the sale of farm land to be turned into subdivisions.

The thought of our nation becoming almost totally dependent on foreign countries for our supply of food crops and livestock products is not something I want to ever seriously contemplate. It is beyond frightening to me and should be scary for any intelligent, thinking person. As the farms disappear, the independence and spirit of our nation dies with them. In a very real sense, farmers and ranchers in this country are under siege. God help my grandchildren if the radical environmental and animal rights groups succeed with their objectives. Both groups should be able to find common ground with farmers and ranchers without the need to portray all of our country's livestock producers as villains.

When we bought our land, Stormwind Farm was planted in soybeans, a crop that the anti-livestock crowd approves of. I know without a doubt that the farm's environment is in better shape now than when we moved here. Except for small amounts of weed killer sprayed underneath the fence lines, we have not applied harmful chemicals to our soil. During the summer, yellow jackets unfortunately must be killed near the barn areas and the house. These particular wasps can become very aggressive in their attacks on humans or animals. I wait until dark and spray their nests. No other insecticides are applied anywhere on the farm.

The pastures are fertilized with composted manure, organic manure tea, pelleted organic fertilizer, and lime. I frost seed white clover most years. Like all legumes, clover draws nitrogen from the air and deposits it in the soil. Our soil has improved tremendously over the years. It is so healthy and full of earthworm activity that an agricultural specialist advised against using an aerator on the pastures.

"Your pastures don't need it," he pointed out, "your soil is in terrific shape."

Soil health ensures the health of the alpacas and all the other creatures on our small farm. I believe that our healthy farm environment attracts a more diverse wildlife population each year. Stormwind Farm is a tiny community of humans, livestock, dogs, and many other critters. We all try to co-exist the best we can.

Claudia and Rupert

Chapter 10

ALPACA MAMAS

It is common for dairy farmers to take newborn calves away from their mothers when they are only a few hours old. In some cases, this is done right after birth. The calves are fed colostrum and milk replacer with a bottle until they are old enough to grow and gain weight on pasture, hay, pelleted feed, and whatever else dairy producers deem suitable. This management system maximizes milk production and profits for the farmer. Or so is the general belief.

What are we to think then of organic dairy farmer, Harry Lewis, from Sulphur Springs in Texas? According to the author of *Deeply Rooted*, Lewis allows calves to suckle on their mothers until they are naturally weaned. Lisa Hamilton asked Harry's son, Wynton, to explain this seemingly odd management system.

Wynton had what Hamilton described as a simple answer: "Mamas do a better job raising them than we do."

Wynton's father later explained that "the calves suckling helps their mothers ward off mastitis, an inflammation of the udder that is the bane of dairy farmers everywhere" (Hamilton). Harry Lewis sells his milk to an organic co-op. Although it's not explicitly stated, the cows, despite nursing their calves, produce enough milk for the Lewis farm to turn a profit.

I loved Hamilton's book because it tells about independent thinkers and farming with common sense. The farmers, who thought "outside the box," were not afraid to question conventional wisdom. None seemed to worry about the approval of their contemporaries. All cared deeply about their land and their livestock.

I fully share Harry Lewis's beliefs in the importance of pasture for grazing animals and in allowing the mamas to do a good job raising their babies.

At Stormwind Farm, I respect the instincts, the knowledge, and the innate good sense of the alpaca mamas. The longer I know these amazing animals, the more important it becomes to me to show them my trust in their judgment.

Of course, the alpacas are dependent on me for their food and drink, but I show faith in their ability to otherwise manage their lives. While I ultimately decide which animals are sold and which ones get to stay, I don't view the crias as "mine" while they are still strongly bonded with their mothers.

Very early on, I understood that acceptance by the herd boss, Breeze, would be my ticket to acceptance by the larger herd. Make friends with the herd boss, and the rest of the herd will become much easier to handle!

When I enter the barn, I don't think of it as my barn. It's Big Mama's house! I get to clean it, scrub the water buckets, and stack the hay. Breeze makes the rules. She's fine with my close physical presence. Because she trusts me and permits me to stand close to her, the other females follow suit.

When I purposely walk away from a newborn cria to go drink a cup of coffee in the house, my departure communicates trust to the baby's mama. "Your baby is beautiful," I tell her, "but you don't need me now because you know what you are doing."

Sometimes, I discreetly observe a birth from the front porch with the help of binoculars. If everything goes smoothly, I intervene as little as possible. In any case, no female on Stormwind Farm gives birth alone. The other females are there to lend a hand, so to speak. First-time mamas especially can use a little moral support from their herd mates. Just having the herd close by makes them feel more secure and confident. But it's much more than mere moral support. Friends, mothers, adult daughters, or sisters help out in so many ways. For example, inquisitive sniffing and gentle prodding by the herd often encourages a newborn cria to get up and nurse.

The alpaca females check out Caramel's newborn cria.

Unlike our Whippet bitches, alpacas don't lick their babies to dry them. Additionally, canine mamas stimulate urination and defecation by licking each puppy's anus as well as vulva or penis. You never see the meconium because bitches eat it along with the placenta. I have never observed an alpaca female show any interest in consuming a placenta. Despite hearing that alpaca females don't actively stimulate urination and defecation of their crias, I see contrary evidence. Here's the interesting part: It's almost never the cria's mama but the other females that lick to move things along.

Sometimes, females too young to be bred act as nannies. Pearl and Libby helped care for Sanibel's firstborn cria, Hunter, even though they had never given birth themselves. It is not unusual for an alpaca nanny to flip up a cria's tail with her nose when she sees the cria make contact with its mama's teats. This stimulates nursing. I've observed this again and again; it's not an isolated behavioral pattern.

Friends of ours owned a female that took helping a newborn alpaca one step further. Doug and Lori Hellman in Colden, New York, had an imported female named MasterCard on their farm. By the time I met

MasterCard, she was a tiny, old lady with more than a few infirmities. Doug and Lori had removed her from their breeding program, but MasterCard was still very much an active member of their herd. One of her daughters gave birth to a female cria that took an unusually long time trying to latch onto a nipple. MasterCard watched her granddaughter intently as one clumsy attempt after another failed to make a connection. Finally, she couldn't stand it any longer.

"What are grandmas for?" she asked, adding, "child, let me give you some help here, or you're likely to starve to death."

With that, MasterCard stepped forward. Using her head and neck, she pushed her granddaughter closer to the target and then expertly guided the baby's mouth towards the nipple. The baby started nursing. Satisfied that all was well, MasterCard resumed eating from the pile of hay laid out in the barn.

There are many alpaca breeders in this country who will never witness such a tender moment on their own farms. That's because they isolate females in labor and those with newborns from the rest of the herd. On some farms, a female alpaca barely gets to touch its own newborn. The farmers take over. The cria is dried with a towel, mucus is sucked from its nose, the navel is disinfected, it is weighed, and its temperature is taken. There are alpaca farmers who administer enemas to help pass the meconium. Others routinely administer antibiotics or inoculations to a newborn cria. Meantime, millions of wild camelids—vicuñas and guanacos—take care of birthing chores without human interference.

Women especially are often terrible micromanagers. At the first sign of birth, their motherly instincts go into overdrive. Here's a confession: I am one of them. The only difference between me and the human helicopter mamas hovering over "their" newborn crias is my very strong belief that human interference with normal birth and newborn care is wrong. I respect and love my alpaca mamas too much to insult them by pushing them out of the way and taking over. I fight my strong urge to meddle and interfere and remind myself with each new birth, "You are not the mama. Back off!"

The cup of coffee that I drink in the house after briefly checking a newborn cria? It helps to give mama and baby time to bond without the distracting presence of a two-legged "midwife." As my understanding and appreciation of alpaca behavior deepened, I found it easier to take the role of quiet observer and be content with that.

Over the years, I've heard of way too many alpaca females that showed fear of their newborns and would not care for them. Was it really fear? People often fail to appreciate an important trait of prey animals. In the wild, it's vitally important for the offspring of prey animals to get up and be mobile soon after being born. Any sickly, weak, or slow-witted baby is a huge liability and poses danger to a herd. It's much safer to let it die and move on. Domesticated prey animals often still have that survival instinct. If an alpaca mama senses that her cria is not right, she may not want anything to do with it. "Not being right" may only mean having human scent all over its body. That scent would come from all the things breeders are busy doing to these little ones when they should be in the house polishing the silver or cleaning out their closets. Or how about skirting all the fleeces that are piled up in the garage?

The absurdity of it all hit me while browsing through a livestock catalog. One page advertised several items that promote the acceptance of a lamb or goat kid by a foster mother. Authors of livestock books usually also offer tricks on how to get a ewe or doe to nurse a foster lamb or goat kid. The catalog items and tricks of the trade invariably deal with fooling the foster mother's sense of smell. It's obviously a well known and accepted fact that livestock mamas don't want to adopt babies with a "foreign" scent clinging to their little bodies. Why do so many alpaca breeders have a problem understanding that alpacas may reject crias whose fleece is permeated with human scent? I have no answer to that question.

I also have no interesting and harrowing tales to report from my experiences at Stormwind Farm. There are no heartwarming stories of how I—the dedicated farmer—saved rejected but plucky newborn crias from certain death. The Stormwind females are wonderful mamas. My services are neither required nor requested. I am free to go clean those closets after a cria has been born.

Of course, I'll assist in an emergency. When one of Breeze's daughters suffered an allergic reaction to a rabies vaccine, the medication our veterinarian gave her temporarily dried up her milk. I bottle fed the cria for one day. Mama and a very hungry baby were totally fine with that. I gave several liquid doses of the herb Fenugreek to stimulate Mariah's milk production, and the very next day, everybody was back to their old routine. Mariah was feeding her cria, and I was minding my own business.

Special herbal formulas are available to stimulate milk production in alpacas. I don't quite understand why they are such a big seller. If alpacas are healthy, not stressed, and fed properly, no milk stimulating supplements should be required. I've seen herbal mixtures given to alpacas that may cause abortions. Mariah was not pregnant when I gave her Fenugreek. On Stormwind Farm, we have never found it necessary to use any kind of milk stimulants except in the incident described above. Even old Breeze still has plenty of milk.

In any case, the animals and I have an agreement. I've promised the alpaca mamas that I will not meddle in newborn care and how they raise their offspring. They know that they can trust me to stay true to my word. When the crias are six months old—and I start handling and training them in earnest—their mothers reciprocate and allow me free reign. It's an agreement born of mutual trust and respect.

At times, the alpacas remind me of many of my former students who, unsolicited, shared family tales and secrets. Alpaca behavior can speak volumes about the way humans treat the animals. It often reveals the presence of a human meddler in their lives. For example, a few years ago, I visited another farm where the animals sent me a clear message about how they mistrusted their care-takers. The owners had decided to close their alpaca breeding operation. I was mildly interested in purchasing a female and went to look at the herd. After casual scrutiny, I was ready to examine two particular females more closely. Their fiber looked beautiful from a short distance.

A wild and prolonged chase now ensued within a fairly large pen until the owner cornered each female and put it in a headlock. These females were yearlings, well past weaning age. Both of their mothers raced up and attacked the owner. Their furious screams rang in my ears as I fled the farm. Back at Stormwind Farm, I felt like I had escaped alpaca hell and entered a sanctuary.

Camelid mothers can be tough if provoked. Llamas, the much larger cousins to the alpaca, have been known to attack and stomp dogs to death that threatened their crias. While vulnerable prey animals are willing to abandon a sickly and weak baby for the greater good, they are equally willing to protect healthy offspring from predators, often with disregard to their own safety.

Maybe you have to be a mother yourself to relate to the fierce protectiveness of many animal mothers. As a child, I was truly puzzled by stories about mothers who sacrificed their health and even their lives to ensure their children's safety and survival. There were many such stories from World War II. "Wouldn't your own will to live be stronger?" I thought to myself at the time. My son, Ben, was only a few hours old when I completely understood a mother's willingness to give up her own life so that her child may live. Human mothers are not the only ones with such feelings, or call them instinct if you prefer.

On Stormwind Farm, the females and their crias live on the two largest of our four pastures. The upper pasture is their winter home, the lower pasture is grazed from May to December. They all share the same spacious loafing area in the barn. I mentioned in a previous chapter that there are no age groupings among the females on our farm. I am not aware of any wild camelid species that separates its females into any kind of groups. Yearling males are tossed out and live in bachelor herds while females of all ages remain together. That makes sense. Young females observe the older alpacas' behavior during mating, birthing, nursing, and raising their offspring. Cross-generational teaching and learning going on in the pastures as well as in the barn continues way beyond the care alpaca mamas and nannies give to newborns. Actually, the give and take between the generations never stops throughout an alpaca's lifetime.

"Isn't that a little far fetched?" a doubtful visitor questioned me once when I talked about alpaca generated lessons on our farm.

I don't think so. Breeders of other grazing species have made similar observations. Jill Ott, an employee of the United States Department of Agriculture in New Jersey, gave me an excellent booklet called *Foraging Behavior: Managing to Survive in a World of Change*, written by Dr. Frederick D. Provenza. Subsections are titled *Mother knows best* and *Advantages of social learning.* The booklet has several terrific stories about learned grazing behavior. Montana rancher Ray Banister shared how the young calves were able to learn from their mothers how to thrive under a new management grazing system. Iowa bison ranchers Bob Jackson and Sharon Magee told Dr. Provenza that bison family units are necessary for proper management. "Young animals benefit from the knowledge of social behavior, food, and habitat selection of older generations," Dr. Provenza wrote. In the book's preface, Dr. Larry D. Butler calls Dr. Provenza's research "new discoveries." This made me laugh out loud. I am convinced any old shepherd living and traveling with his flock of sheep in Scotland could have given us this information. The same goes for nomadic livestock herders as well as observant farmers and ranchers all over the world.

The female herd at Stormwind Farm is often in flux but nevertheless an organic unit, with the old herd boss influencing and shaping herd behavior. Breeze is an individual with uncommonly good sense. She does not start quarrels but is keenly aware of her role as the alpaca in charge. *She who must be obeyed!* Breeze's crias learn early that "no" means "no" and mama will not change her mind. By contrast, we had a boarded alpaca whose crias regularly threw temper tantrums and always got their way.

Overly permissive mamas of any species are not doing their offspring any favors. A good example was Jock. This male cria had been a coddled mama's boy from birth. Whatever Jock wanted, Jock got. The results of his permissive upbringing were only too evident at weaning time. Previously, I never had major problems when it was time for weanling males to leave the female pasture. Most were more than happy to join the boys. All were properly submissive to the older males. They in turn considered it below their dignity to even acknowledge the little pipsqueaks.

Not so when Jock joined the ranks of the big boys. Spoiled rotten, he had trouble understanding that the adult males did not view him as the anointed king of the pasture as his doting mother had. Things got decidedly ugly when Jock refused to make the submissive gestures that mature alpaca males expect from youngsters. When he spit at Tasman, it was the last straw. The normally mild-mannered Tasman was outraged. With menacing gestures, he advanced on the now-frightened weanling. A chase ensured. Tasman pursued the screaming Jock, determined to pummel him into submission.

I was secretly thrilled over this display of much-needed discipline. It didn't last long. Jock's new owner happened to visit and begged me to put a stop to the "poor baby's" screaming. "Poor baby" my foot! Against my better judgment, I moved the brat to a different pasture.

Jock is a gelding now and lives as the undisputed king in a pasture with females and crias. He's still pretty full of himself and has no respect for the breeding males on the other side of the fence. Jock got lucky. In general, young alpacas that act like brats toward their elders are poorly tolerated by the herd.

Over the years, I've noticed an interesting phenomenon. The same mama will often discipline her various crias within a wide range of severity. She'll be strict to the point of harshness with one cria, only to be much more relaxed and indulgent with the next. I can't say that I always see a reason for the change in behavior. Because mamas know best, I butt out.

In the case of Jock's mama, she obviously didn't know what was best for her son, but her behavior seems to be an exception among alpaca mothers. It is in my herd.

Alpaca mothers have a significant impact on how their offspring view humans and interact with them.

"How come your alpacas are so friendly?" more than one visitor has asked me. "Why don't they run away?"

There are several reasons. I've explained most of them already. There is one more, and it's a very important one. Alpacas don't have arms and hands to reach out and touch one another. It makes sense to keep my own arms and hands to myself as I walk among the animals in the barn and on the pastures. My respectful reserve builds trust. When I do touch the alpacas, for example while administering inoculations or de-worming medication, they seem to understand that it's a necessity and the unwelcome contact will be brief. The crias observe their mothers' calm acceptance of my presence in their lives and imitate the modeled behavior.

In addition to Breeze, we presently house seven other breeding females of our own on Stormwind Farm. Then there are the two boarded alpacas, Pearl and Libby. During the breeding season, the herd may be joined by an additional two or three females that are sent here to be bred. Their owners have their own farms but may not have a stud male or simply wish to branch out into other bloodlines. We often sell females with a free breeding to one of our males; those return to the home farm as well. They usually stay for three months. At that time, a loss of pregnancy is no longer likely. The visiting females receive the same loving care as our own alpacas. It's all a lot of work, but it's work that I find to be a pleasure and very rewarding.

Although our animals enjoy good health, it hasn't all been smooth sailing in the female pastures. It never is when pregnancies and births are part of a farm's routine. Disappointments are bound to occur on any breeding farm.

Over the years, we suffered the loss of a few crias. With one exception, I've never lost one that was born alive. I am very proud of that record. The cria that died was born at least three weeks prematurely. The owner agreed to a plasma transfer. Despite medical intervention and all my efforts, the cria succumbed to infection after two days of struggling to survive.

Luckily, our losses have been remarkably few. Only two cases required veterinary assistance.

Dr. Bill Pettit, one of the veterinarians who attends our herd, expertly and with amazing speed "fixed" a uterine torsion using an old but proven method. Our alpaca was gently lowered to the ground and laid out flat. A long, wooden board was placed on its belly. While one of Dr. Pettit's assistants knelt on the board to press against the uterus, Dr. Pettit and I lifted up the female's legs and flipped it on to its other side. The procedure corrected the torsion and saved our alpaca from having to undergo a Caesarian section. Unfortunately, the cria, a beautifully formed female, was born dead. Thanks to Dr. Pettit's skills, its mother easily conceived again two months later and has since given birth to several crias without problems.

A few years later, a male cria died in its mother's womb. It belonged to Claudia. A terrific production female, Claudia always gets pregnant on the first breeding and retains the pregnancy. Her babies pop out of her generously built body as easily as a slice of toast out of a toaster oven. Last year, I realized something was wrong as soon as her second stage labor started. Only one leg protruded from the vulva, and nothing else happened for fifteen minutes. Luckily, I was able to reach Dr. Nancy Lee. She arrived on the farm within minutes of my phone call. An internal examination revealed that Claudia's cervix had not opened properly. Despite the bad news, we had one very important factor in our favor. Dr. Lee is a petite but strong, young woman. Her arms and hands are tiny. The song *Thank Heavens for Little Girls* wasn't written with veterinarians in mind, but the title applies to what happened on our farm that day. Using skill, strength, and incredible patience, Dr. Lee managed to manually dilate the cervix enough to pull out the cria. Any female that experiences dystocia is prone to a uterine infection. Claudia therefore received several prescribed doses of antibiotics. Like Mariah, Claudia also conceived again without further intervention, a tribute to Dr. Lee's expertise.

Both females were totally cooperative during their ordeals. Claudia in particular is not very fond of human attention and can get easily riled. Despite the pain she suffered, she showed her appreciation for my help. Hours after I had already disposed of the dead cria, Claudia remained by my side. Repeatedly, she nuzzled me and pressed her face against mine. She would never do this under normal circumstances.

People sometimes ask us why we use the services of two veterinarians. In this area of the country, large animal veterinarians are a rare species. They are often busier than they want to be. The majority only want to treat horses. Dr. Lee has a large equine practice. She works mostly on race horses. Dr. Pettit owns a clinic for dogs and cats in addition to caring for alpacas, llamas, sheep, goats, cows, horses, and any other critters that cross his path. I don't think he'd refuse to work on any animal, no matter how exotic or rare. We're fortunate to have two knowledgeable veterinarians to call for routine care as well as in an emergency. If one is busy, we've increased the odds of getting service by having a back-up to contact.

Most births don't require any help, and that's as it should be. I look forward to each one. The excitement over a new cria never becomes old. The alpacas share my feeling. I've noticed that the very first cria born in the spring on Stormwind Farm is always virtually mobbed by all the females. They can't get enough of looking at it. They sniff and nuzzle it repeatedly. Libby exchanged baby kisses with Pilot after he was born even though Pilot is Bella's cria. Their tongues darted in and out of their mouths with lightning speed and made contact. This went on for several minutes. It's a very common alpaca ritual. Some breeders theorize that mamas use it to "seed" their crias' digestive systems with good bacteria. I think that's a valid theory. Whatever the reason, the gesture is endearingly touching.

Several years ago, I read a fascinating book with the title *Songs of the Gorilla Nation*. The author, Dawn Price-Hughes, is autistic. Like all autistic people, she had difficulty interpreting human social behavior. Working closely with a small group of gorillas at a zoo gave her the opportunity to observe the primates' social interaction. In her book, Dawn Price-Hughes gives examples of how her studies of gorillas led her to a better understanding of human behavior.

I don't doubt the authenticity of Price-Hughes' claims for one minute. Alpacas are neither humans nor primates, but people who think they're mere fiber factories on four legs couldn't be more wrong. Observing the rich social lives of the alpaca mamas and their offspring often gives me pause to think. I am not autistic—and the brains of prey animals are not wired the same as those of predators—but living with alpacas has immeasurably deepened my own understanding of human nature. Above all, it has opened my eyes to the amazing level of communication that is possible between the members of different species. The alpaca mamas of Stormwind Farm have my respect and my affection.

A cria enjoys a sunny day in the fall.

Chapter 11

CRIA SONGS

In my opinion, alpaca crias—like human infants—are not particularly attractive right after birth. They're soaking wet from amniotic fluids, and their fiber is tightly plastered to their skinny bodies. Bony and gawky looking, a newborn alpaca usually weighs around fifteen pounds. At both ends of the spectrum, there are tiny survivors of ten pounds or less and strapping whoppers of twenty-five pounds. I hope never to see one in the latter category on our farm. High birth weights are not desirable in any livestock species due to an increased chance of dystocia.

Within twenty-four hours, the homely, leggy newcomer morphs into an adorable, fluffy creature. Alpaca crias are doubtless among the most endearing of all baby animals. The charm and just plain cuteness of a little alpaca are hard to resist. I experienced an example of this early on during our days as alpaca breeders.

Who can resist the charm of an alpaca cria?

Building a house on our newly-purchased farm took up an enormous amount of David's and my time. Friends generously fostered the two youngest of our Whippets—Stormy and a little bitch named Hannah—for almost an entire year. They raced and coursed them and gave the little dogs the attention they craved. My friend Marie felt keen disappointment that our travels with Whippets had come to an end. Several times she used the term "stupid alpacas" to describe the animals that fueled my new passion.

Our second cria, Mariah, and the first to be born on Stormwind Farm, was a week old when Marie paid us a visit. After we finished lunch, I cajoled, "Come on, let's go see the alpacas."

Marie reluctantly agreed. As we left the porch, the animals were nowhere to be seen. We approached the barn from the dog yard and entered it through the service door.

"Where are they?" Marie asked with little enthusiasm.

"Go out the barn door, they're probably behind the barn in the pasture," I said as I encouraged her to walk ahead.

Following along, I paused to check the water bucket. Suddenly, I heard, "Ooooh—" followed by a long silence. When I investigated, I found Marie and Mariah staring at each other. Harley hovered nearby, visibly nervous about the stranger checking out "his" baby. Breeze kept a wary distance. She wore the haughty expression that she reserves for most humans who visit her home. During the first years of our relationship, I was often the recipient of Breeze's queenly scrutiny. Apparently, I've been judged acceptable because she has not given me the hairy eyeball in a long time.

Marie and Mariah were unaware of Breeze's disapproval. They remained standing motionless for quite some time, each entranced by the other's presence. There was no more talk about "stupid alpacas" after their encounter. Marie wasn't around when it came time to halter train Mariah. I think she would have been surprised to see how quickly alpacas can learn a new skill.

On Stormwind Farm, all crias are initially conditioned to quietly accept being handled and wear a halter. After that, they are also trained to cooperatively walk on a lead. Because of our small breeding program, I can afford to indulge my crias.

Large livestock operations normally do not train their animals to accept a halter and walk on lead. For example, most cattle and sheep are herded into an enclosure and then a chute for inoculations and other treatments. At the end of their lives, they are herded from feed lots to the designated slaughter area.

Traditionally, the only individuals in a livestock herd to receive much handling and training are animals shown as 4-H projects or breeding stock exhibited in sanctioned shows. I don't know whether alpaca farmers with large herds follow this management model. Those who own small herds like us halter train all their crias, at least the farm owners I am personally familiar with.

Four women have had an impact on how I treat the crias growing up on our farm. Carol Masters was the first to impress on me that alpacas are prey animals and don't respond to humans in ways we have come to expect from fellow predators, our canine companions and friends. Carol's explanations were the foundation for what slowly evolved into a comprehensive program.

The next woman to help shape my philosophy on handling and training was Dr. Temple Grandin. I found her book, *Genetics and the Behavior of Domestic Animals*, when I researched color genetics in mammals. This was years before Dr. Grandin became the famous "rock star" of the livestock industry. She's a remarkable person. In any case, at one point, Dr. Grandin discusses an interesting phenomenon found in rats. First, she explains that "development of emotional reactivity of the nervous system begins during early gestation." Later, she cites research which showed that handling pregnant rats and stressing them created nervous offspring. The study also showed that briefly handling newborn rat pups helped in developing a calmer temperament.

Of course, alpacas are not rats, but I reasoned that both species have similar physical reactions to fear.

At Stormwind Farm, we handle pregnant females only when necessary and with calm gentleness. Crias are touched briefly after birth and in weekly sessions that last only a few seconds. They are never chased or grabbed roughly. I've placed two catch pens in different areas of the pasture. Alpaca crias are very curious and will often enter a newly opened catch pen to investigate. When a cria does that, I take the opportunity to restrain it lightly for just a few moments. Halter training begins when crias are around six months old.

The last two women who have had a profound effect on how I work with our alpacas are Marty McGee Bennett and Dorothy Hunt. Marty is the founder of *Camelidynamics*, a program based on the philosophy and teachings of Linda Tellington-Jones and her *Tellington TTouch* program.

Dorothy Hunt is the first *Camelidynamics* practitioner to be certified by Marty.

The *Camelidynamics* program differentiates between handling and training. When we handle alpacas, we simply expect them to stand quietly while things like inoculations are done to them. Nothing is expected of the alpaca except to stand still. Training involves active participation from an alpaca, such as walking alongside the handler after being haltered. Several management procedures straddle the areas of handling and training. For example, when I trim toenails, the alpaca stands in place but is also expected to cooperate by holding up its foot.

Two Camelidynamics workshop participants practice haltering techniques.

Dorothy, who teaches a *Camelidynamics* workshop on Stormwind Farm each year, has changed the way I handle and train the alpacas as compared to the early days. For example, halter training can be a time of frustration for many owners, an unpleasant chore that must be faced with grim determination. I feel joy and a special, emotional connection with my animals during training.

Very much like human children, no two crias are exactly alike in personality. Their reactions to humans and training differ widely. Two of our crias were amazingly quick to convince that wearing a halter and walking on a lead are fun things to do.

Those two were Riverman and a very nice, little female named Memphis. Riverman, in essence, taught himself. He accepted the halter without showing fear and appeared quite comfortable wearing it for the first time. I stepped a few feet away from him, turned my back, and waited patiently. My posture was relaxed and my breathing calm and steady. This is always my first, brief lesson with halter and lead. It gives the baby a chance to think and gather its wits before I give further instructions. Most crias don't automatically get the idea that they can walk normally while wearing a halter and with the lead connected to a human. Riverman hesitated for less than a minute. With my back turned to the cria, I sensed rather than saw the little alpaca's first, cautious steps toward me. "That's a good, good boy," I praised him profusely, and away we went. That was the extent of Riverman's training.

Memphis, whose mother can be so difficult, was just as easy to train. Before I halter a cria for the first time, it is accustomed to being gently restrained with a special catch rope designed by Marty McGee Bennett. I don't proceed until the cria reacts with total nonchalance to this procedure. Memphis was so calm and cooperative the very first time I used the catch rope on her that I immediately progressed to fitting the halter. I clipped on the lead. Memphis looked up at me expectantly. "We're going for a walk," I explained in a friendly tone of voice. A tiny tug on the lead, a step forward, and Memphis followed. I had never lead trained a puppy with such ease.

Jacalyn, who boards her animals with us, had the same pleasant experience when she trained Libby, her very first alpaca. Libby was the perfect cria for a novice owner. Jacalyn was to have a much more difficult time with Pearl. I've come to the conclusion that Pearl is highly intelligent and prefers to set her own agenda. She wants to be the one in charge. Luckily, Jacalyn is a patient and intuitive woman. Pearl certainly put her patience to the test! Crias that want to lead rather than follow are, in my experience, more difficult to train than the frightened ones that are frozen to a spot in sheer terror.

I've described two extremes. Most crias will fall somewhere in between. Without exception, all will be helped by the thoughtful methods of the *Camelidynamics* program.

By chance, I discovered an additional, magical technique to help me handle and train not only crias but also adult alpacas that are unusually fearful. I should thank the author of the book that added another dimension to my program. Unfortunately, I recall neither the book's title nor the author's name. All I remember is that it was a book about the history of the American cowboy. The author explained that cowboys sang to their cattle to calm the animals and prevent dangerous and costly stampedes. Is it true that cowboys sang while circling the grazing and resting herds at night? I don't know, but what I read left me thoughtful and pondering my handling and training of alpacas. If singing calmed cattle, why shouldn't it work for nervous alpaca crias? Who would know if I tried it and was not successful? Only the alpacas would be witnesses to my failure, and they'd never tell.

Alpaca crias that are very scared usually do one of two things. They either freeze or turn into whirling dervishes at the end of the lead. Singing gives confidence to the former and calms the latter. When I sing to a frightened cria, I use a monotone, soothing "sing-song" voice. Sometimes, I make up words as I go along. Oddly, I often find my choice to be a song from my childhood in Germany. My favorite—and the one that works best—is a haunting, melodramatic ballad about two royal children who fell in love but were unable to reach each other across a wide stream. I continue to be amazed at the effect this song has on crias that are normally too scared to concentrate on anything but their fear. Those rooted to a spot suddenly walk behind me as nicely as you please. The ones thrashing on the ground or doing flips at the end of the lead soon stop the hysteria.

These magical results remind me of an old German fairytale called *Der Rattenfänger von Hameln*. It's the story of a rat catcher who becomes angry at the citizens of Hameln when they try to cheat him. He takes revenge by bringing his flute to the market place. As he starts to play, the boys and girls of Hameln gather around him and eventually follow him out of town. The parents never see their children again. These kind of stories were popular long before the age of political correctness. Of course, the "children" I sing to are always returned to their alpaca mothers at the conclusion of each lesson.

In the beginning, I sang only to the crias during halter training. Eventually, it occurred to me that my technique would work just as well with crias that were nervous, for example, during inoculations. Success! "Why stop here?" I thought. By the time a boarded adult alpaca, Pamela, was scheduled for an ultrasound, I had gotten over any embarrassment I may have felt earlier. "Why should I feel self-conscious if my methods bring comfort to animals?" I thought. Nevertheless, I considered it prudent to warn Dr. Lee about the strange concert she was about to witness. I am not an accomplished singer.

"This female is new to the farm and still very nervous," I explained as

Dr. Lee set up her ultrasound equipment in our barn. "I'll be singing to Pamela to keep her calm," I added.

The unflappable Dr. Lee didn't even blink. "Oh, O.K.," was all she said.

The haltered Pamela was brought into the darkened barn. I loosely tied her lead to a stall panel. As I gently held her in balance, Dr. Lee started her work. I could feel Pamela's body go tense. She made nervous snorting noises and hummed in alarm. Very softly, I started singing little nonsense songs, telling Pamela she was a beautiful girl and would soon be free again to join the herd on the pasture.

Pamela relaxed. Instead of standing high up on her toes, she settled back into a normal stance. She lowered her neck, and her breathing became calm and steady. Soon, Dr. Lee was finished with the examination. Pamela stood still while I slowly removed her halter.

At first, I was reluctant to share the stories of my cria songs with other breeders. Now I don't care. The cria songs work. We talked about the songs during last year's *Camelidynamics* workshop held on Stormwind Farm.

"Yes, I know they work," one participant agreed. "We have a female with an infected foot. The infection needs to be treated every day. My husband does it, and he sings to our girl the whole time he's putting on the ointment. It keeps her calm."

I am not sure why the thought of singing to soothe the crias did not occur to me earlier. It works with human infants. Unfortunately, modern parenting no longer includes loving mothers singing lullabies to help their babies fall asleep.

It is Dr. Temple Grandin's belief that music is part of our evolutionary roots. In *Animals in Translation,* she not only discusses birds, the obvious musicians in the animal world, but also the songs of humpback whales.

Alpacas use a spectrum of sounds to communicate with one another. Mamas hum to their crias and vice versa. Adults hum when they are nervous or frightened. Females often "talk" to one another for comfort and reassurance, for example while one herd member is giving birth. The most vigilant of the herd members sound a shrill alarm call if they detect a person, an animal, or an object they perceive to pose a danger to the herd. Alpaca males orgle during the mating ritual. Some females refuse to cush and submit to a silent suitor.

When the young daughter of a fellow breeder heard the farm's herdsire orgle in the breeding pen, she called, "Mom, come quickly, Sasha is singing his song."

I find it interesting that the little girl perceived the orgling as "singing." No wonder my alpacas are so responsive to what I call cria songs.

Music can have a hypnotizing effect. Army generals knew this. It's no accident that generations of infantry soldiers marched into battle and to their deaths to the rhythmic cadence of drums and even entire bands playing. Why would alpacas not be mildly hypnotized by the sound of cria songs? They are, after all, mammals like us.

Gifted handlers and trainers have apparently always used singing to communicate calm reassurance as well as praise to their animals. Long before I knew what an alpaca was, an English trainer named Henry Blake sang to horses for the same reasons that I sing to my alpacas. He wrote a book about his training methods. The title is *Talking With Horses*. It was published in the USA in 1976. I find it strange that the English queen, a superb horsewoman, paid so much attention to a North American trainer called "The Horse Whisperer" when she had a homegrown "whisperer" living practically under her royal nose. In his work with horses, Henry Blake described using the same monotone "sing-song" voice I use with alpacas. Without knowing it, I was practicing methods identical to those of a successful English horse trainer!

Far away from England, on another continent, a livestock herder used the technique to communicate with a bird. He had never heard of Henry Blake. Karen Blixen, who wrote under her pen name Isak Dinesen, told the very moving story in *Out of Africa*. On her Kenyan farm in the African Highlands, Blixen had a German cuckoo-clock. At noon each day, the little Kikuyu boys—called totos—used to leave their goats and sheep in front of Blixen's farm house to watch and listen to the cuckoo as it sprang out of the clock's innards for its midday call. One tiny toto came back by himself some days, stood in front of the clock, and talked to the cuckoo in a slow sing-song voice. It is immaterial that the solemn, little fellow didn't realize that the wooden cuckoo was not alive. He was a true animal "whisperer" and most assuredly sang to his goats and sheep. Blixen repeatedly mentioned in her book how passionate the Native Kikuyus felt about their livestock.

In *Talking With Horses*, Henry Blake came across as a practical, hardworking man, with definite goals of what he wanted to accomplish with the horses under his care. He did not appear to be given to fanciful dreams and hysterical thoughts.

Nevertheless, he firmly believed in extra-sensory perception (ESP) as well as telepathy when it came to working with horses. ESP is the transfer of moods and feelings from humans to horses while telepathy is the transfer of mental pictures. I agree with Henry Blake that both ESP and telepathy are possible between members of different species. Individuals must be open to this type of communication. They must be in the right frame of mind. I do think that there are many imposters and charlatans in this field who only have the gift of gab. That's unfortunate because I am convinced that the true gift exists.

The subject of communication between humans and animals is fascinating in its full complexity. Why do some people instinctively have the ability to connect with animals, to understand their motives, and to interpret their behavior? Why are others so oblivious to what animals are trying to tell them? The second group includes people who like or even profess to love animals. They certainly wish them no harm yet often show an utter lack of understanding animal emotions and behavior.

Dr. Grandin, who is autistic, believes that because people with autism view their environment differently than "normal" people, it is easier for them to access the world of animals. She gives examples of how autistic people see small details that, for example, cause cattle to react fearfully in a slaughter facility. I don't doubt that Dr. Grandin is right, but I feel intuitively that autism is not a prerequisite to understanding and communicating with other species.

I am convinced that many people—autistic or not—have the innate ability to master cross species communication skills but are simply not willing to do so. Surely one reason is the common attitude that humans rule over the animals under their care, and it is not up to the rulers to learn the language of their subjects. Additionally, our fast-paced and very noisy environment has dulled as well as overwhelmed our senses to a point where the often quiet and subtle language of prey animals escapes our notice.

Over the years, I've noticed how many people are uncomfortable in a quiet room with no distractions. Cria songs will not work if the singer does not rest peacefully within herself or himself. You cannot soothe others if you are not calm yourself.

There is a component of my management program for which I have not found an effective way to communicate verbally with the alpacas. When I wish to confine the alpacas in a small area for various procedures, I must either lure them with food or use a herding tape to direct them into a catch pen. I was therefore fascinated to read about a high-pitched vocal technique called kulning. I have not heard the kulning sound and don't know whether it resembles the yodeling practiced by herders in the various European alpine regions. It has been used for centuries by female Swedish shepherds to communicate with cattle and other grazing animals. Traditionally, the herding calls— kulning has no lyrics—are practiced by Swedish women who accompany their animals to distant pastures from May to October. The sounds carry over several miles. The women use kulning to gather the animals at night, or when it's time to move on to another pasture.

There are people who think this is all romantic nonsense. That's their loss. I have a fairly good understanding of why the cria songs work. I am not sure why my crias seem to respond to the story of the two separated royal lovers more so than to other songs. As the story unfolds, the prince drowns during the attempt to reach his love. When a fisherman finds his corpse, the princess enters the water to end her own life. Not long ago, I translated the verses for a friend born and raised in this country.

"Good Lord, they had you kids singing this morbid tale at summer camp?" Linda shook her head.

They certainly did—and usually around the camp fire at night. I still remember the quiet afterwards. Those camp counselors were no fools!

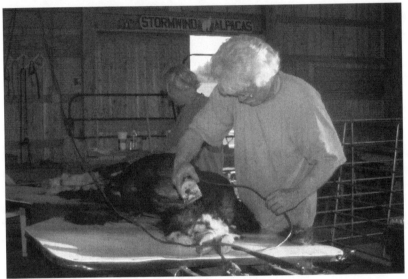

David shears a very pregnant Bella.

Chapter 12

SHEARING DAYS

Most alpaca farmers who hire a professional shearer expect him or her to finish the job in a single day. Many shearers therefore travel with a support crew. Working with several helpers, an experienced shearer can easily finish a herd of twenty alpacas in three hours or less. That includes setting up and taking down all the equipment. A young and strong crew often spends barely ten minutes removing the fiber from one animal. Good shearing crews are much in demand. The wise alpaca farmer schedules the fiber harvest months in advance of the actual event.

It's a far cry from what happens on Stormwind Farm during shearing time. Our goal is to finish three alpacas each day. If we feel especially energetic, we may shear four, but that's rare. The whole process can be dangerous to animals as well as people. Alpacas are not as easily restrained as sheep. David and I are both in our sixties. At that age, your strength and reflexes are far from their peak. I want both of us to be physically and mentally fresh to ensure a good and safe job.

"Look at the time you spend!" cried a fellow alpaca breeder.

"Look at the money we save," I replied.

This year, I could reasonably expect to pay $650 to have twenty alpacas shorn by a professional crew.

There are several other distinct advantages to shearing our own animals. We like to start the last week in April. Because we don't have hired help, we can be flexible and adjust our schedule depending on the weather. Severe cold or rain pushes the beginning of shearing into May. Instead of watching our shorn alpacas shiver, we simply cancel a shearing day. No big deal! We can wait for warmer weather and for fleeces to dry. Weather can cause havoc with the tight schedule a professional crew must follow. We escape that potential cause of stress.

Another important consideration is biosecurity. Traveling shearing crews can bring all kinds of diseases to a farm. A big issue is infectious skin diseases, such as mites or ringworm. Some crews do an outstanding job of disinfecting equipment, but not all are fastidious and super careful. When we do our own shearing, we don't have to worry about biosecurity at all.

There are several different ways to shear alpacas. We've tried a few over the years. Finally, we settled on a method that works for us and gives me great fleeces to sell to hand spinners and other fiber artists.

Prior to being shorn, alpacas must be restrained. Again, there are several options on how to accomplish this. Each restraining technique has its merits. There is none that's best for every single shearer.

Our alpacas are restrained and shorn on a professionally fabricated tilt table. The alpaca selected by us for shearing is haltered, and a lead is attached to the halter. The table top is adjusted to a vertical position. A large belly band that's attached to the table is securely fastened around the alpaca's middle. The table top is tilted to a horizontal position. Because an alpaca can use its long neck for leverage, I immobilize it with a clip attached to both the halter and a metal ring welded to the table's corner. The alpaca's legs are then gently stretched and fastened to metal extensions that can be adjusted to each animal's size.

All of this has to happen with the speed of lightning to avoid any kind of serious struggle. We prefer a third person to help us but have restrained and shorn quite a few of our alpacas without such assistance and without tranquilizing the animals.

"Are the males hard to shear?" questioned my sister, Karin, during a visit to our farm.

Well, they're not. Our males are usually very cooperative.

"The hardest ones to control are the pregnant females. Understandably, they are the most nervous," I explained.

With each shearing season, though, an alpaca learns to trust us more not to hurt it.

Since shearing is something we only do once a year, a little warm-up is needed on the first day to polish rusty skills. We usually start with Dexter. He's the oldest alpaca on the farm and has been through the drill numerous times. At his age, his fiber is too coarse and too short to sell. There's no need to be super careful to get the best results. All David has to do is brush up on his techniques and not nick Dexter with the very sharp and therefore dangerous shearing blades.

Once Dexter and the other two oldies, Breeze and Harley, are shorn, we're down to serious business. I sell every ounce of the usable fiber produced on Stormwind Farm. David knows this and works hard to help me maximize the income from our annual fiber harvest.

Before he starts shearing, however, it's my turn to blow dust and debris out of a fleece. I use a very powerful, commercial blow dryer to do that important job. Unlike sheep fiber, alpaca fiber has no lanolin and is dry. The animals take frequent dust baths and, for health reasons, should not be prevented from indulging in this practice. Dust penetrates all the way to the skin. Very fine fiber catches lots of debris. Cria fleeces are the worst.

"You're driving the dust deeper into the skin with your blowers," a professional shearer told me.

Not with my management system! I spend at least ten minutes blowing out dust from the exposed side of the body. By the time I'm done, there isn't a speck of dust left in the fleece or on the skin. After the initial shock, all our alpacas relax and enjoy the breeze. It must feel good.

When Jacalyn helped us shear the first time, she asked repeatedly, "Are you sure you didn't give this alpaca a tranquilizer?"

Although I had not administered one, I understood why she asked. The males were utterly relaxed and practically asleep on the table during dust removal.

Professional crews will usually not permit the owner to blow out the fleece while the alpaca is on the table. That's understandable. Shearing is a seasonal business, and time is of the essence. Luckily, time is something we have. An even better way to manage dust removal is a vacuum system which sucks rather than blows the dust out of a fleece. This is especially true if a fleece is to be shown. The vacuum technique allows the lock structure of a fleece to remain intact. We tried a standard shop vacuum cleaner. It wasn't powerful enough and didn't give good results. A giant commercial system is cost prohibitive for our small herd. This is not a problem. For processing purposes—raw fiber to yarn—a blower works perfectly well.

Finally, the blower is shut off and set aside. David begins to shear. There's a real art to good shearing, and shearers follow a specific pattern. Techniques can vary among individual shearers. The most important goal, aside from safety, is to wind up with a fleece of uniform staple length. The shearer's hardest task is to avoid second cuts, the bane of all fiber processors. Second cuts are very short pieces of fiber. They are created by running the blades over a previously shorn section of the body. A few second cuts are almost unavoidable and can easily be removed during skirting. Many second cuts ruin a fleece. No hand spinner or other processor will be interested in purchasing such a fleece. David and I had lots of arguments about second cuts until he watched me skirt a fleece. Then he understood and cooperated.

In 2010, we had the rare pleasure of having two helpers during two of our shearing days. John and Kristin Thorpe now offer shearing services to other alpaca owners.

While David shears, I harvest and store the fiber. The blanket—the fiber from the main part of the body—goes into one bag. That's the prime fiber and the most desirable. The coarser neck and leg fiber is scooped into another bag. Again, our aim is to harvest fiber for production purposes. It is of no importance to us to remove the fleece in one piece. That technique must be applied by breeders who plan to enter a fleece in a show. For our purposes, removing the shorn off fiber after each pass of the shears works well. Once all the fiber has been harvested, David switches to clippers. They give the fleece remaining on the animal a nice, smooth looking finish. We've received many compliments on how our alpacas look after they've been shorn.

Now it's time to lightly loosen the leg restraints, remove the head clip, and flip the alpaca over onto its other side. Once the restraints are tightened and the head clip is fastened again, the entire process from blowing out dust to the final clipping is repeated.

When David is finished, it's my turn again. First, I trim the tail fiber and top knot with hand shears. Next, I trim toenails with pruning shears and check between the toes for thrush or any other abnormalities. The skin was already checked during shearing and clipping. I inspect the inside of the ears for any kind of problem. The last check for a male is a quick look in its mouth. If fighting teeth have erupted in a young male, we file them down to a nub right then and there.

Finally, the restraints are removed, the table is quickly tilted back to a vertical position, and the shorn alpaca is gently deposited on a thickly padded mat. I remove the halter, and a much cooler and more comfortable alpaca steps out of the shearing area. We clean table and floor and are ready for the next "customer." The entire process takes about forty minutes, much longer than the brief time spent by a professional shearing crew.

From my observations, professional crews leave more fiber on an animal than we do. Many breeders ask for leg fiber to remain on the alpacas. One visitor to Stormwind Farm told me that our slick-shorn alpacas looked like "weird Dr. Seuss characters." I think they look beautiful, especially those with excellent conformation. Caramel, in particular, looked gorgeous this past spring after shearing. With her feminine head, long legs, and slender yet muscular body, she reminded me of an elegant ballerina. In any case, all the fiber grows back.

Caramel

Potential buyers who are not accustomed to looking past a shearing job they don't like may miss out on a good or even great animal. One year, a novice breeder visited our farm and saw a young male we had purchased. The alpaca had been slick-shorn the previous week. The visitor fell silent as he looked at Prince.

"Are you disappointed? He doesn't look like much," the fellow finally commented

I smiled. "Oh, I'm very happy with him," I responded truthfully.

Many months later, the same visitor showed up at the farm again, only this time it was several weeks prior to shearing. The alpacas were in full fleece by then, with good to great staple length and full leg coverage. The man's eyes popped open when he noticed Prince.

"Who's that?" he asked with obvious interest and admiration.

"That's Prince," I answered and couldn't resist a little teasing, "remember, you didn't like him at all."

The man lapsed into shocked silence. Finally, he said, "That's amazing. He looks so much better from when I saw him the last time."

It's true, Prince had filled out and become more mature, but he did not look "better." His conformation and fiber had the same great qualities a year ago; our visitor had simply not been able to look past those slick-shorn legs and trunk.

Occasionally, just the opposite happens. Too much fiber, especially on the lower legs, can create an unfavorable optical illusion. Years ago, as superintendent of a small show for shorn alpacas, I came across the pedigree of a young, black male. Bella Cria's Good Fortune had been bred by Hugh and Carol Masters and was now owned by a young couple with a farm not too far from us. I liked Derek and Deborah and was happy that they had entered the show. Fortune was only six months old. Had I ever seen him? No, not even in a photo, but I had seen and admired a few of the alpacas in Fortune's impressive pedigree.

It sounds a little foolish, but sometimes I get good vibes about a situation. My gut feeling told me to act on my impulse to inquire about this male.

"I just have to see this little male, and it has to be today," I announced.

David looked at me with surprise. We had not discussed purchasing another male.

"Well," David grumbled, "it's only time and money for fuel. I guess a look isn't going to cost anything."

With happy anticipation, I picked up the phone and dialed the Lamer's number. Deborah answered.

"Yes, you're welcome to come look at Fortune," she responded to my request, "but we're shearing today. If you want to see him in full fleece, it'll have to be within the next two hours. We'll shear him last."

Less than an hour later, we walked into the Lamer family's barn and found Deborah, her husband Derek, and a friend busy shearing one of their female alpacas. A little black male stood next to its mother in the back of the barn.

"That baby has crooked legs," David whispered. "Will they straighten out?" he wondered.

"Be quiet and have patience," I whispered back and counseled, "let's wait and see."

Luckily, the noise from buzzing shears in the background had blotted out our clandestine conversation.

Deborah walked over and encouraged us to take a closer look at the cria. I touched Fortune's fleece. It was incredibly soft and had a slick, almost wet feel to it. Even in the somewhat dimly lit corner of the barn, I saw the luster and brightness in Fortune's black fiber. The little male's body was sturdy and compact. The fiber on its legs was heavy, reached all the way to its toes, and yes . . . the cria appeared to be a little knock-kneed.

"Look, I've got to go and drive our babysitter home," Deborah announced. She directed her husband to shear Fortune in her absence. "I'll be back in a few minutes," Deborah promised.

Derek and his friend went to work. Derek sheared with nice, easy passes while I scooped Fortune's fiber into the bags Deborah had prepared prior to her departure. There was a lot more fiber than I had expected to see from the tiny cria. I was impressed. Derek was almost finished.

"I'll just trim Fortune's top knot and tail," he announced.

With mounting horror, I watched the transformation happen right in front of my eyes and felt powerless to stop it. After all, I didn't own Fortune and couldn't very well dictate shearing techniques to the person who did own him.

Zoom, zoom—a few passes and Fortune's beautiful, thick top knot was reduced to a short stubble. Zoom, zoom—and the bushy fiber on the cria's tail was gone, leaving an almost bare, little rat tail. Derek released the leg ties, and Fortune sprang up from the shearing mat placed on the ground. Oh my! The former proud and beautiful little alpaca male looked like . . . what? A comic book creature? The head—minus the top knot—seemed miniscule in size, the ears hugely out of proportion and bat like in comparison. The bare little rat tail hung down limply. Fortune, to say the least, looked pathetic and not at all attractive.

My eyes moved down to the shorn legs. A big smile spread across my face. "I hope the price is right," I thought to myself. Fortune's legs were perfectly straight. With all the fiber gone, that was plain to see.

Deborah had returned and showed only mild shock over her husband's handiwork. I looked again at the tiny, bat like creature and smiled at Deborah. "I'd like to buy him," I said.

Two years later, the little black male with the bad hair cut was a beautiful adult alpaca and became Halter Champion Bella Cria's Good

Fortune. He has truly been a good fortune for Stormwind Farm. Not only is he beautiful, he has a terrific personality and is one of the most likeable alpacas I've come in contact with. Fortune has high fertility, his breeding behavior is impeccable, and his sons and daughters are beautiful.

I can thank my instinct—but mostly my years raising Whippets—for my decision to purchase Fortune. Evaluating dogs taught me that first impressions can be deceiving. A poor grooming job can distort an animal's looks so as to make it unrecognizable. That's not true of Whippets, which have a naturally smooth coat, but during my travels and because of my friendship with other breeders, I had plenty of exposure to heavily coated canine breeds and kept my eyes open.

Poor Derek had to endure my teasing him over his shearing job. It had been his very first time shearing an alpaca. Derek's skills have much improved over the years.

I can say the same for David and myself. Shearing is not fun for us, but we learn new things and improve our management skills with each shearing season. It's exhausting, often dirty, potentially dangerous but ultimately satisfying work. A farm must have a purpose and produce a harvest. Our alpacas produce fiber, a useful as well as beautiful agricultural product.

After the last alpaca has been shorn for the year, I always allow myself a few days of rest. Only routine, daily chores are performed during the respite. Then it's time to tackle the somewhat tedious but informative business of skirting the shorn fleeces.

Why is skirting informative? The intensive handling of the many fleeces I've skirted over the years taught me a lot about fiber quality. Not surprisingly, a fleece also reveals the health status of an animal. For example, disease or stress can cause alpacas to develop stress breaks in their fiber. Lack of minerals as well as poor nutrition in general can change the color of a fleece.

Professional skirting tables are very expensive. Many alpaca breeders build their own. Because we take so much care in blowing out dirt and debris prior to shearing, I don't need a skirting table. I spread my fleeces on our dining room table to remove second cuts, the rare wisp of hay, and other imperfections.

Since 1997, the very beginning of our fiber harvest, I've sold every ounce of fiber produced on Stormwind Farm, with the exception of the fiber I've used myself. I bought a spinning wheel but never passed the stage of rank amateur. My knitting skills suffice for the creation of scarves and hats, but that's about it. Is it any wonder that I prefer to sell my fleeces to fiber artists? Most are sold raw to hand spinners. Occasionally, I'll send fiber to small commercial mills to be turned into yarn, rovings, and felted sheets. What a pleasure it is to have a customer show me a beautiful sweater or vest knitted from the fiber harvested from our alpacas! Felted sheets have been turned into beautiful wall hangings. You don't have to be skilled yourself to appreciate the amazing talents of true fiber artists. The variety and quality of products created by these gifted women and men is mind boggling.

Carol Masters created these attractive and warm alpaca hats and scarves.

Carol Masters is such an artist. Her lacy shawls, felted hats, and other pieces of clothing fashioned from alpaca yarn are as exquisite as they are practical. Each garment is unique.

"I love working with alpaca fiber from your farm," a knitter once told me. She added, "What I really like is knowing how well the animals are cared for and how gently they're treated."

Her comments made me feel good about what we're doing on our farm. Like many of our customers, she also appreciates that the raw fiber as well as the yarn are produced in environmentally friendly ways. I am proud that alpacas from Stormwind Farm contribute to our nation's supply of natural fiber products.

Black-eyed Susans and zinnias are Ingrid's favorite summer flowers.

Chapter 13

THE FOUR SEASONS

Imagine living in a climate without seasons! I would not care for such boring sameness. The changes in temperatures and all that comes with them define the year for me, if not time itself. Each season has things to look forward to and its own special rituals and traditions. New Jersey has four distinct and separate seasons even though they overlap at times. Living and working on our small farm has given me a unique perspective. I don't think of spring, summer, fall, and winter as beginning and ending according to the Gregorian calendar. Instead, I define the seasons as to what happens on the farm. On the Stormwind calendar, the first day of spring is not on the twentieth of March. Rather, spring has arrived when the soil warms up and new grass sprouts in the pastures, regardless of the date. It's spring when the forsythia bushes are blooming, and when it's warm enough to work outside without wearing a jacket and a hat.

On Stormwind Farm, the arrival of spring means keeping a close watch on pregnant females about to give birth. Females due in the spring often carry their fetuses longer than those scheduled to give birth in the fall. The duration of an alpaca pregnancy normally varies between 335 and 359 days. It's not unusual, though, for spring pregnancies to extend well beyond that time frame. A long gestation period may mean a very large cria and a difficult birth. Regardless, spring babies are special. People are tired of winter by then. Spring births represent new beginnings and renewal of life. The alpaca females themselves are "hungry" for a newborn cria in their midst.

As soon as the weather warms up, males start showing off in the hopes that their fighting prowess will dazzle the open maiden females. It does! Or, at the very least, it interests them. The females gather at the fence line and intently watch the male wrestling matches. Some cush at the fence, indicating their willingness to be bred.

During mild days in April, I open those barn doors that have been kept tightly closed during snowstorms and windy winter days. Our alpacas are never locked inside their barns. One barn door is always kept open. Nevertheless, by the end of the winter, both barns need a good airing out. Bedding straw and any old hay is raked outside and spread on pastures or dumped in the compost bins. The floor mats are swept and scrubbed with soapy water. A clean and tidy barn floor helps to keep fleeces clean prior to shearing. The less hay that sticks to fiber, the less work I'll have during skirting. Feed containers are cleaned and put in the sun to dry. After shearing, the service areas of both barns are given a good spring cleaning. Finally, the heated water buckets are put away and the summer buckets taken out of storage.

In our part of New Jersey, the spring season seems to be getting shorter each year. During some years, you're barely aware that it has arrived, and it's already gone to make way for summer. Of course, there are the unexpected late frosts to discourage the overeager gardener. Our first spring on Stormwind Farm, I was so determined to garden that I ignored my Golden Rule of planting time. A severe frost in early May destroyed all my work. After that rude shock, I wait until Mother's Day each year to put out seedlings and plant seeds. You just never know what weather extremes will come along during springtime in New Jersey.

The middle of May is often already uncomfortably warm, and the beginning of June may be brutally hot and humid. I consider the first day of summer the day I hose down the alpacas to cool them off. Regardless of what the calendar says, when David attaches garden hoses to the water hydrants in the barns, I declare, "Today is the first day of summer."

It's the least restful season of the year on the farm. In New Jersey, summer heat waves are invariably coupled with high humidity. That's a dangerous combination for alpacas. Even shorn alpacas can suffer from heat stress. The alpacas spend much of their day time in the barn during the summer season. Most of their grazing is done at night, a complete reversal from their normal routine. The large barn fans set at floor level help a great deal with keeping the alpacas happy during the day. I add extra water buckets in each barn and check them several times throughout the day. During extreme heat waves, I literally monitor the animals every hour and offer a cooling spray to those who wish to take advantage of this service.

If we force animals to live in a climate that is not natural to them, we should at the least do everything to make them comfortable. Summer is therefore definitely a "stay at home on the farm" time for me. My friends know that I will rarely accept an invitation for an extended luncheon date or a visit away from the farm during hot days. A whole day spent away from the farm without a farm sitter is totally out of the question. I know that many others alpaca farmers work full-time during the summer and find ways to keep their animals cool. Since I have the luxury to stay home with mine, I take advantage of it.

By the beginning of June, I've skirted all my fleeces. It's an activity I enjoy. After all, fiber is the final product and the ultimate purpose for raising alpacas. As I already explained in the chapter on shearing, the intense handling of so much fiber has taught me a lot about fiber properties and how to evaluate fiber quality. On many farms, bags filled with fiber are stored in garages, basements, spare rooms, or even barns. With a busy spring and summer, it's easy to put skirting fleeces on the back burner, so to speak. I purposely leave all bags with unskirted fleeces sitting in our living room. It's an incentive to complete the task.

On Stormwind Farm, birthing and breeding starts in late April and ends in late November. Fellow breeders are sometimes horrified to discover that I don't suspend breeding during the summer months.

"Why do you breed when it's so hot?" one asked. Before I had a chance to respond, she exclaimed, "It's horrible for the alpacas."

No, it's not, at least not with my cooling program. The full body soakings prevent heat stress, infertility, and abortions caused by high temperatures. I soak a male immediately after breeding, paying special attention to the scrotum. Of course, like all breeders, I prefer mild and sunny days for reproductive activities. Who wouldn't?

Unfortunately, it's not just the alpacas that are breeding during the summer months. Flies and mosquitoes step up the pace of procreating during warm weather. I make sure there's no standing water to encourage the growth of our mosquito population. The farm's natural fly predators are supplemented with fly traps. Bait stations go up in the spring but need to be emptied and refilled more often during the summer.

Of course, summers in New Jersey are not all about heat, flies, and humidity. There's the locally grown produce that tastes delicious. Juicy tomatoes, green and red hot peppers, many varieties of corn on the cob, sun-ripened peaches . . . it's all fresh and grown on farms of the Garden State. New Jersey strawberries and blueberries are yummy treats, either eaten "pure" or served with pound cake and whipped cream. There are huge watermelons and cantaloupes, and let's not forget the famous zucchini that everybody grows and then curses because of the huge surplus nobody wants. With the exception of blueberries, we've grown all produce on Stormwind Farm at one time or another. I grow only enough for ourselves and to share with friends. Over the last few years, I've neglected the vegetable garden. This year, I am determined to plant one again, albeit reduced from its original size. While I weed the garden and harvest its bounty, I can't help but remember that summer used to be my preferred season. As a young girl, I loved hot weather. Baking myself in the sun was a favorite summer pastime. Now that I am much older, I prefer cool or even cold weather. So do the alpacas. We are well-suited to one another.

Would I sacrifice the fall season in the Northeast so as not to suffer the heat of the summer? Not a chance! Fall is beautiful! The beginning of September ushers in warm, sunny days without humidity. The nights are cool. The air conditioning is shut off and windows are thrown wide open. The alpacas probably feel like they're in Heaven.

"Look at them," David says, "it's like they never come up for air."

He is talking about their constant grazing. They are busy, busy, busy! Flakes of orchardgrass hay are spread in the barn and on pastures, but they are rarely touched. There is lots of freedom and good exercise on spacious pastures for little alpaca tykes. The crias run and play all day, with occasional naps in the midst of lush, green forage. They nibble playfully on the pasture without any real interest in grazing. Their mothers have plenty of milk, and the little ones have full bellies from nursing.

The black-eyed Susans and purple cone flowers have gone to seed. Purple cosmos still bloom brightly in the large flower bed next to the farm lane. Deer browse contentedly among the wildflowers in the buffer zone next to the wetlands.

Fall is my favorite season for singing cria songs. Dorothy Hunt visits Stormwind Farm and presents her annual *Camelidynamics* workshop in the fall. Every year, she has something new to teach me and the other workshop participants.

Fall is also a great time to attend festivals and farm markets with alpacas and alpaca products. In our early years, hardly anyone could identify an alpaca. Now most people are at least vaguely familiar with the animals and clothes made from alpaca fiber.

Attending a festival with alpacas is a great opportunity to educate the public. It's also very exhausting. Parents are not always concerned that their children are respectful of the animals. Sometimes, it's hard for me to be patient at the end of the day. We never take females or very young crias. Tasman and Fortune are the best candidates for public education. They're big enough so that rowdy teenage boys—the worst offenders when it comes to rude behavior—feel enough fear to keep their distance. At the same time, the alpacas are tolerant when toddlers laugh and scream in their ears. Tasman and Fortune are both cool under pressure. One year, I took Riverman along. He, too, was a perfect officer and a gentleman.

By the end of the day, though, the alpacas are all always happy to climb back into the trailer. Home! Away from the crowds, the noise, and the confinement of the small livestock pen! Back to their pastures and their peaceful existence at Stormwind Farm—where a stray cat stalking field mice past the fence may be their only visitor on a given day. I am always happy as well to return to the solitude and quiet of the farm.

On some days, the only people I'll see are those traveling over our pastures in a hot air balloon. They lean over the basket and wave. I wave back and call a loud, "Hello." Once, when the large female pasture was still a hayfield, a balloon landed in its center. When I went over to greet the crew, the balloon's pilot gave me a bottle of champagne.

In late fall, the burning bushes on Stormwind Farm turn bright red in earnest. I planted lots of them, a whole row along the parking area near the house and more behind the dog run and near the pastures. At the height of their showy beauty, the color of their leaves is aflame as if on fire. When the leaves fall and only the red berries remain to feed the birds during the cold months, I know that winter will be here soon.

To some people, late fall is a sad time of the year. True, there are rainy days with a melancholy air about them, but those are not necessarily bad. Reflections on endings and a little sadness at times are normal feelings. Nowadays, many people seem to think that, unless they are happy and joyful every single moment of their life, there is something wrong with them. Those are unrealistic expectations.

To me, late fall is the beginning of a restful period for humans, animals, and the soil. Much as I enjoy gardening, I also appreciate the break I get from planting and weeding. Much as I love breeding alpacas and seeing crias born, by late November I look forward to the more sedate pace between December and April. Late fall is the gentle transition from the busy fall season to the quiet winter months. There is color again, for a brief time, with bright orange pumpkins and dazzling displays of mums decorating porches and beckoning from farm stands.

The song birds start to gather now to fly south. At times, it seems there are a thousand of them sitting in a huge pin oak next to the upper female pasture. When they leave the tree and gather on the ground, the alpacas' home is literally black with birds. The noise is deafening. The alpacas have become accustomed to the sights and sounds and are no longer nervous and agitated. The insistent honking of the wild geese flying in V-formation over the farm does not perturb them either. It's a final warning call that winter is around the corner.

By the middle of December, sun and wind are no longer strong enough to dry out the lower female pasture after a rainfall. When we purchased the farm, we had drain tiles installed. They work well, but there's a limit to what they can do on our heavy type soil. It's all a mixed blessing, as are most things in life. When other alpaca farmers complain about the sun burnt stubble in their pastures during July and August, our alpacas graze contentedly on green grasses and legumes. We do not irrigate. It's not necessary. The downside is that the lowest pasture is too wet to graze for four months out of the year. There are ways to address this problem but—for one reason or another—none have been tried yet.

The beginning of winter therefore heralds the grand entrance of the herd into their winter pasture. It is located on the highest elevation of our rather flat land. Water runs off to the now vacant summer pasture. Alpacas, like sheep, love to enter a "new" pasture. The grass is always greener on the other side, right? In some cases, of course, it truly is. Open the gate, and the entire herd of females and crias races and pronks around the field in an excited frenzy.

By now, the visiting females that were here to be bred to Stormwind males have been sent home, along with their crias at side. The reduced herd size is a good fit for the smaller winter pasture.

My friend Marie calls December through February "the dead months." "I wish I could hibernate like a bear," she says.

Winter may be a quiet time on the farm, but there is no time to hibernate. Some days, it seems that I am busier than ever. Composted manure must be spread on the fallow pastures not occupied by the alpacas.

"So, where is your manure spreader?" a visitor asked recently.

I grinned and held out my arms. Quite simply, I shovel manure from the compost bins into a wheel barrow, dump the load where I want it, and spread it with a large rake. There's not enough manure to justify a mechanical spreader. We don't have the space to store one. Most important, the large summer pasture is too wet to allow a vehicle on it at the very time the manure needs to be spread. I've noticed that the spread manure disappears faster with each passing year. That's because our soil has become healthier and more fertile with each season. The increase in beneficial soil bacteria, dung beetles, and earthworms accelerates the disintegration of manure.

In February, I frost seed white clover into those pastures that need a little help with extra nitrogen. Graziers call clover "green manure." I wait until snow is in the forecast, and the ground is frozen solid. Clover seeds are very tiny, which makes them ideal for frost seeding. The heaving of the soil—freezing and thawing in intervals—works the seeds into the soil. Come spring, the seeds germinate into a healthy stand of beneficial legumes. Popular belief among alpaca breeders considers the consumption of clover to be harmful to the animals. I have not found this to be true. Of course, my pastures do not just grow clover but contain lots of other plants as well. I always offer hay free choice but make doubly sure it's available when the clover is especially lush in the spring. During that time, David also mows to keep pastures clipped short.

The first time I frost seeded, David was more than a little embarrassed to see me do it the old-fashioned way. I pour the seeds into a bowl and spread them by hand with wide, sweeping motions. I get nice and evenly spaced out coverage that way.

My husband became angry when I refused to let him use the large spreader hooked up to our mower. "Don't you feel silly spreading seeds by hand?" he asked.

To the contrary, I felt that his question was a silly as well as a strange reaction, but then David is not a farmer at heart.

I do everything I can not to compact the soil. That means keeping machinery off our pastures as much as possible. It's perfectly fine, though, to frost seed a pasture while the animals are walking on it. More than that, it's actually helpful. The hooves, or, in the case of alpacas, padded feet, work the seeds into the soil. Frost seeding is one of the most peaceful activities on the farm, and one that makes me feel very much rooted to the land. There is no way I would spoil my enjoyment with a noisy tractor or mower to pull a seed spreader.

In addition to spreading manure and frost seeding, I trim trees and bushes while they are dormant during the cold months. Yes, farm work continues right through the winter months. While some days are very busy, the farm's work load is lighter than during the other seasons. By January, I've run out of excuses for not having washed windows and tackled other housewifely chores.

Ingrid and Mariah walk on Stormwind Farm on a winter day.

The alpacas graze throughout the winter. When snow covers the ground for several days, they become a little cranky and seem not quite sure what to do with themselves. On sunny days, I spread hay for them on top of the snow. With no fresh pasture plants available, the alpacas' mineral consumption increases considerably.

The only winter weather conditions I truly fear are those that produce a solid sheet of ice on the ground. It's very easy for an alpaca to slip and fall on ice. For that matter, it's very easy for an alpaca farmer to slip and fall. Several friends of mine suffered nasty injuries while tending to their farm chores. I don't allow visitors—not even prospective buyers—on our pastures while the ground is covered with ice. Luckily, in our area of New Jersey, icy conditions like that don't occur very often.

Sure, it gets cold during the winter season. During our first years on Stormwind Farm, I didn't want to wear a nice alpaca hat and alpaca gloves to work outside. A minor but nevertheless somewhat painful case of frostbite in my hands and feet convinced me of my foolishness. Now I'm well prepared for brutally cold temperatures: alpaca socks on my feet, alpaca gloves on my hands, and an alpaca hat on my head!

The farm is quiet during the winter. We don't get many visitors looking to buy alpacas during that time of the year. Friends and family come, of course, but they seldom venture out into the barns or pastures. They live in cities and towns and are not used to the biting wind blowing across our open pastures.

The Whippets hate the cold as well and refuse to stay outside except to go potty. My mother, who was an excellent seamstress, sewed little red coats for them during her last visit to Stormwind Farm. I've never known a Whippet to dislike wearing a coat during cold weather. They are very much like cats in that they love warmth.

The alpacas wear their own, natural "coats." Cold does not bother them. They'll even cush outside during frosty, windless nights. When I look out the window in the morning, I see that their fleeces are covered with white crystals.

When it snows or the winds howl and whip angrily across the pastures, most alpacas prefer to eat and rest in their draft free, cozy barns. I miss seeing them in their pastures. During those evenings, I often sit longer than usual on an overturned bucket in the barn and observe the alpacas chew their cud. It's a good time for mulling things over; I think about how lucky I am to live a lifestyle I always dreamed of.

As I said earlier, I like and appreciate all the seasons. Each has something special to offer. Even before moving to the farm, I was very much aware of seasonal changes. As a child, I spent most of my free daylight hours playing outdoors. As an adult, I embraced activities such as hiking and gardening. The Whippet races and lure coursing trials I attended were all held outdoors. My dogs and I were active during rain, heat, frost, and even snow. It still amazes me at times to hear alpaca breeders complain about weather conditions that left Whippeteers of all ages completely unfazed.

The alpacas have added another dimension to my level of seasonal awareness. No wonder that I pay little attention to the Gregorian calendar. The seasons on Stormwind Farm begin and end with the natural rhythm of nature. Although the length of each season therefore varies from year to year, there is a predictable and comforting sameness to the seasons themselves. For sure, there is never a "dead" time or a boring or non-productive time.

I am very grateful.

Ingrid and Dexter

Chapter 14

DEXTER

Dexter was born on the fourth of December, 1994. His owners at the time were Hugh and Carol Masters of Serenity Alpacas. Hugh and Carol eventually cared for up to seventy alpacas—both suris and huacayas—on their farm in Hunterdon County in the New Jersey Highlands. On the day of Dexter's birth, however, they owned only a handful of huacaya alpacas. Dexter's registration certificate—issued by *Alpaca Registry Inc.* (ARI) when we transferred ownership into our names—lists him as Medium Brown/White. (The original certificate was issued by the *International Lama Registry* (ILR). This was standard procedure until alpaca breeders started their own registry.) The color designation does not begin to adequately describe Dexter's rich, red fiber covering most of his upper body as well as his extremities. There are white markings on his neck and muzzle and a tiny white spot on his forehead.

Dexter's pedigree traces back to some of the early Chilean imports. The only great-grandsire listed on the pedigree, Uber's Sampson, was imported into the United States from England. Many novice alpaca breeders are under the impression that the country of import is where the animal was born and raised. That's not necessarily true. Because of foot-and-mouth disease in Peru and Bolivia in the 1990s, U.S. government regulations made it difficult to bring alpacas from those countries to the North American continent. More relaxed and less expensive quarantine protocols therefore restricted imports of South American alpacas to those originating from Chile for many years.

Peruvian and Bolivian breeders did not export their camelids to the U.S.A. until the more stringent import requirements were lifted. This did not always stop all of them from sneaking alpacas across the borders into Chile. In *The Complete Alpaca Book*, Eric Hoffman relates an illuminating experience in that regard. It's a shame that clever marketers still exploit the "country of origin" issue. I think their success is a reflection on the lack of confidence many breeders have in their own ability to judge fiber and conformation.

In any case, I don't particularly care where Dexter's ancestors—or those of the other alpacas on Stormwind Farm—were born and raised. It's pretty much a meaningless piece of information as far as I am concerned. Of course, I feel grateful to the South American breeders. In our farm's marketing material, I sometimes mention the South American countries listed on my alpacas' pedigrees because buyers want to know this information. I feel quite silly doing so. The U.S. alpaca registry is currently closed to imports.

I don't remember Dexter from our first visit to Serenity Alpacas. At the time, I focused on purchasing a bred female and gelding. I looked at the farm's intact males without any deep interest. Dexter did not catch my attention.

When Breeze and Harley were delivered to Stormwind Farm, Breeze was pregnant with her first cria. She was due in February, not a good time for an alpaca to be born. In later years, Hugh and Carol were very much opposed to winter births and did not breed for birth dates before the danger of severe frost had passed.

Our contract called for them to pick up Breeze in time for her to give birth on their farm. I had mixed emotions about this. On one hand, I was very disappointed to miss the birth of our first cria. On the other hand, David and I worked full time off the farm, and I knew it was in our best interest to allow the move. A winter birth with both of us gone for most of the day? Not a smart plan! Common sense therefore prevailed when we discussed the issue, and we readily agreed for Breeze to give birth at Serenity Alpacas.

"What will happen to Harley?" I wondered.

With Breeze gone, Harley would be left without a companion for possibly several months. Alpacas are herd animals and cannot, or should not, live alone. We were offered the option of sending Harley back with Breeze. I was unhappy with that plan. By now, the alpacas were part of our lives. Taking care of them had become an enjoyable routine. To look at an empty pasture for months would leave a void.

"Would you like us to bring Dexter down to keep Harley company?" Carol asked.

This was more than generous, and I gladly accepted. Dexter arrived, and Breeze departed. While Harley had been gelded for quite some time, Dexter was an intact breeding male. Normally, a gelding is submissive toward an intact alpaca male, but Harley had been the undisputed king of the pasture since his arrival at Stormwind Farm. This title only existed in his own mind. Actually, he was merely the consort to the queen. Nevertheless, Harley was quite puffed up with his own importance. A legend in his own mind, he was not about to relinquish the crown to the usurper.

There were daily skirmishes. Physically, the two alpacas were not an even match. Harley outweighed Dexter by at least forty pounds. He was soon to find out that Dexter was not afraid to throw his wiry, little frame into a fight. My sister, Karin, who was visiting the farm at the time, watched the alpacas' tussles from her bedroom window. Each morning, she gave the daily report at the breakfast table.

"The little one chased the big one again," she'd tell us. "Why is the big one so afraid of the little one?" Karin questioned with some consternation the next day.

Eventually, the two adversaries declared a truce and spent most of the time companionably grazing in close proximity to each other.

Dexter was easy to handle, and I came to enjoy his presence on our farm. We were not prepared, however, to purchase a third alpaca at that time. Dexter would have to depart shortly. Breeze had been bred again at Serenity Alpacas. Soon, it was time for her to return to Stormwind Farm with her cria, Kalita, at her side. Reluctantly, I bid Dexter good-bye. David also liked him and was sorry to see the red alpaca male leave.

The years went by. I saw Dexter during my visits to Serenity Alpacas. He had kept his wiry frame and always looked fit and healthy. One day, we heard that Dexter had been sold to the owner of a new alpaca farm in New Jersey.

"We missed our chance. We should have bought him," I complained to David. He agreed.

Sometimes, there is no logical explanation why a particular animal tugs at your heartstrings. Dexter looked good, but I had seen more impressive looking alpaca males over the years. He had produced very nice crias. One of his sons took a first place in a large class at a huge East Coast show under a very respected South American judge. That was great, but I am not one to be overly impressed by show wins. What can I say? I just liked this tough, little male with the intelligent expression in its large eyes. Our own alpacas kept me plenty busy, but every so often, I'd wonder how Dexter was doing.

During the summer of 2004, Dexter was offered to us. We decided quickly to bring him home to Stormwind Farm. The breeding males at that time were Tasman, Taku, and Mendel. Dexter was close to ten years old then and still in good shape. Of course, he was no longer in his prime. He was nevertheless considered competition by the other Stormwind males and was treated accordingly. Taku and Tasman decided to deny Dexter entrance into their barn. Dexter played it cool. He kept a low profile and avoided confrontations by giving the other males their space and not pushing the barn issue.

"Don't worry, they'll give in within a few weeks," I assured David who became increasingly more worried about the old guy.

I was wrong. August and September came and went. Dexter spent his nights tightly cushed against the outside of a barn wall. The tiny overhang from the roof offered little protection when it rained.

"It's all right," I assured David, "it's not cold enough for the rain to bother him."

By the middle of October, I began to worry as well. Winter wasn't that far off. Soon, we would have to find a shelter for Dexter.

"Those idiots," David railed about the other boys, "why are they so mean to him?"

We finally decided that a miniature barn had to be constructed to keep Dexter and his hay dry during inclement weather. David picked up lumber and other supplies. He spent several days building a sturdy addition onto the existing barn. It is spacious enough to comfortably house two or even three alpacas and has electricity and its own entrance. The boys observed David's hammering and sawing with great interest. When the tiny barn was completed, I named it Dexter's House. We covered the dirt floor with a large rubber mat, and I placed a flake of hay on it. A feed dish and mineral container were added. As a last amenity, I hung a heatable water bucket from a hook in a wall. Satisfied, I surveyed Dexter's new domain.

"He'll be lonely in here," I thought wistfully, "but at least he'll be dry and comfortable." With soft and fuzzy thoughts about my wonderful husband warming my heart, I left the pasture and returned to the house.

At bed check time, there was a light drizzle. It was one of those raw nights we sometimes experience on the East Coast in the late fall. Not freezing cold but wet and nasty; definitely the kind of night when most people don't linger outside any longer than they have to.

"Just in time," I thought with satisfaction. Hopefully, Dexter would have already taken possession of his new house by now. After pulling on rain gear, I headed to the female barn. Quickly, I checked mamas and crias. All was well. I turned off the lights, hurried across two pastures, and peeked into Dexter's House. No Dexter! I had not seen him huddled in his customary spot outside.

"It's dark and raining, I probably missed him," I thought. With a few steps, I arrived at one of the barn doors leading into the boy barn. "Well, I'll be . . . !" I yelled in surprise.

There, in perfect harmony—and looking like butter wouldn't melt in their mouths—sat Taku, Tasman, Mendel, and Dexter. They were chewing their cud, not missing a beat, and showing no reaction to my loud outburst. Shaking my head, I took care of chores and left the barn. There sat the empty Dexter house. It looked so nice and well built. The lovely, little flake of hay inside looked untouched. No mobile alpaca lips had disturbed the smooth surface of the minerals stored in their bin. Fresh water sparkled in the brand new bucket.

"Now that Dexter owns real estate, the other guys respect him and have accepted him," I joked after telling David about my discovery. "It's pretty funny," I added.

"Yeah, it's hilarious," David responded dryly, no doubt thinking about the expense of the barn materials and the hours spent building the shelter.

For a long time, the Dexter House was used as a storage shed. Last fall, I cleared it out to make room for Hunter and Pilot. They will have shelter there until they leave for their new home.

At one time, we took Dexter to the farm of customers. The Campbell family had purchased Fireman Steve, and the plan was to leave Dexter as a temporary or possibly permanent companion. The Campbells had also purchased several suri alpacas from other farms. By chance, a young male named Puck arrived within minutes of our own delivery of Fireman Steve and Dexter. Puck immediately realized that Dexter was old and vulnerable and let him know that he, the great Puck, would be in charge. That's normal alpaca male behavior.

"They'll adjust to each other," I assured the Campbells.

Dexter was grazing in the distance as David and I turned to leave. We had barely reached the pasture gate when Dexter raced to our sides.

"Don't leave me with this maniac," he seemed to cry. Actually, his cries of distress were more like a pathetic whimper.

That's all David had to hear. "We're taking him back home with us," my husband commanded in a firm voice.

There are times when even a strong-minded woman knows better than to argue with her spouse.

I am reminded—no, make that warned—at regular intervals by David that Dexter is "on the endangered species list" and has been placed "under environmental protection." That's in case I should ever feel tempted to sell him, give him away, or put him out on loan again.

Perish the thought! Dexter has carved out a niche for himself as baby sitter and elderly mentor to weanling males. With them, he is once again the big guy in charge, a general followed by his obedient troops! Quite wisely, he remains deferential to the young, mature males as long as they don't try to come between him and his food.

Dexter asks for little. He doesn't put a big dent in the farm's budget. He requires little care or attention. Dexter's teeth are wearing down, but he still grazes well and chews cud. For a while, I kept finding small plugs of wadded-up hay in the barn. I worried that Dexter was no longer able to grind up the hay and digest his food properly. Several inspections of his mouth did not reveal any problems. Luckily, the appearance of the hay plugs stopped.

Some alpaca farmers put warming coats on their old animals. The staple length of Dexter's fiber is considerably shorter than what it was in his prime. The fleece is still pretty dense. Until I see the old man shiver, I will not purchase a coat for him.

Dexter still gets frisky occasionally and engages in a little play fighting with one of the other males. It happens rarely, and it's obvious that the younger breeding males no longer take him seriously.

With good care, Dexter can easily live another ten years. As long as he remains healthy, I hope that he does. I've never believed that breeders or owners should keep their animal companions alive at all cost. Loving owners often cannot face death and therefore pretend that the animal still has "quality of life" even though this is obviously not true. No wonder! Our society has the same problem with human family members. I'll never forget what an old neighbor told my sister. This woman was in her nineties, physically infirm but still of sound mind.

"I want to die," she said, "I've had a good life, but now I'm ready."

My sister remained silent.

"There is only one problem," the old lady continued, "every time I try, my stupid daughter calls the ambulance service and saves me."

If an old and sickly animal could talk to us in a human voice, how often would we hear a similar complaint? To an alpaca, quality of life means grazing, eating hay, good digestion, and living as an accepted member of a herd. By the standards of a very old alpaca, that "herd" may consist of one or two other herd mates. It'll be enough to make it happy. By any standards, Dexter's life still has quality.

I've often pondered our special attraction to him. I suspect that one reason is Dexter's very expressive face. Many alpacas are wool blind. That means that their entire face is completely covered with a dense fiber "mask." Looking at a wool blind alpaca's head, a person sees a round shape of fiber, with only the animal's lips clearly visible. In extreme cases, the animal's vision is severely impaired. This trait is considered a fault by many breeders of fiber producing livestock. Unfortunately, it's thought of as desirable by a few alpaca breeders. If the trend spreads, it will become increasingly difficult to select against it in a breeding program.

In contrast to wool blind alpacas, Dexter has a "clean" face. I have always appreciated this feature. Unfortunately, I did not have a camera on hand to record what happened one spring day.

To give the plants in the smaller of the two male pastures a chance to recover from winter grazing, I allow the males to graze in the dog yard. The latter is really more like a small pasture than a lawn. Of course, while the alpacas graze, I keep the Whippets confined to the house. Since there is nothing in the yard that can harm the alpacas, they are permitted to freely wander around.

One day, I sat at the dining room table. Taking a brief break from working on an article I had promised the editor of a camelid publication, I looked up and gazed out the window at the grazing alpacas. The windows on the lower level of our house are large and reach almost from floor to ceiling. A person sitting at the dining room table is clearly visible from the outside. None of the alpacas had ever shown any particular interest in the house.

Suddenly, Dexter appeared in the flower bed next to the dining room window. I looked on with curiosity as he stepped past the bushes planted near the house. Soon, Dexter's head loomed right behind the window. His nose was pressed against the glass. When he saw me, Dexter's eyes flew wide open. He stared intently at me. Studying the alpaca's face, I could almost read his thoughts. His expression first registered shock, then bewildered confusion, and finally a hesitant acceptance.

I waved and called, "Yes, it's really me, Dexter. Hello there!"

Dexter continued staring at me. Eventually, his expression changed to, "Oh well, how strange to see her in there, but it doesn't seem to be anything to worry about." Finally, Dexter backed away from the window, turned, and resumed grazing.

I don't want readers to think that Dexter is a saint in the disguise of an alpaca male. There are times when he can get impatient while I trim his nails. Each day, I stand guard to prevent him from stealing the pelletized feed from Fortune and Prince. Those are his only, admittedly very minor, vices. Luckily, Dexter seems to have a sixth sense when his cooperation is really needed.

For example, we used him as our guinea pig when we tried shearing on the newly purchased tilt table the first time. The restraining techniques must work like clockwork or an accident is likely to occur. We had never even watched an alpaca being shorn on such a table. On the big day, a helper was not available. The shearing crew consisted of David, me, and old Dexter.

Looking back, I am still amazed at Dexter's level of cooperation that day. It was almost as if he thought, "I better not move. These two fools have no clue what they are doing. They need my help."

Alpacas that are extremely frightened are often frozen in fear. Novice breeders frequently mistake this frozen state for compliance. I was not a novice and knew very well the difference between calm cooperation and a fearful, almost catatonic state. Dexter was calmly cooperative! He lay quietly on the table while David practiced fitting and adjusting the leg restraints. He appeared to be almost snoozing while we held a lengthy conversation about the safest way to flip an alpaca on the table. With infinite patience, he endured our fumbling when it was time to remove the restraints and tilt the table back to a vertical position. Gracefully, he slid down to the mat and jumped nimbly to his feet. David and I looked at him with pleasure and relief.

"Old Dexter, he's my man," David said.

Mine, too!

*Emily Stacy and her suri alpaca, Chiquita, wait to
participate in a 4-H performance class.*

Chapter 15

Alpacas as Livestock and Pasture Companions

Alpacas have been bred for thousands of years to produce fiber for garments and household goods such as rugs and decorative wall hangings. They are classified as livestock by the United States Department of Agriculture. Originally considered exotic animals in North America, alpacas are slowly becoming accepted as domestic fiber producers, along with sheep, goats, and rabbits.

There are many reasons why people buy, sell, breed, raise, and board alpacas. Before purchasing an alpaca, it's prudent to explore all options. Potential owners should try hard to find the answers to the following questions: Why do I want to own alpacas, what do I intend to do with them, and will I expect to make a profit?

As income-producing livestock, alpacas can be divided into two sub-categories: seed stock and fiber animals. Farmers may choose to breed alpacas—and sell adults as well as crias—as seed stock to other breeders. Others may elect to breed and sell alpacas to farmers and fiber artisans who wish to maintain fiber herds without producing additional offspring.

Presently, I do not know of any North American breeders who breed with emphasis on a superior carcass for meat production. I don't doubt that alpacas are slaughtered for personal food consumption on some farms.

The breeding and selling of livestock is not for the faint of heart. It is a physically, mentally, and emotionally demanding occupation. Much study and thought should go into the establishment and subsequent management of a breeding farm. Breeding any livestock species is a very complex undertaking. A large expenditure of money does not qualify a novice breeder as an expert. There are no instant experts, much as some breeders like to think there are.

People without any prior livestock experience rarely realize that they don't know just how much they don't know. In other words, many breeders don't become aware of their glaring lack of knowledge until the animals are already on their farm, and they feel overwhelmed by problems or even routine care protocols. To avoid potential disaster, novice livestock breeders should seek a mentor with at least several years of experience breeding alpacas. An ethical mentor will literally spend hundreds of hours with a novice alpaca farmer over the course of the first few years. It is therefore fair to either purchase alpacas from the mentor or agree to pay a consulting fee.

Breeding farms vary considerably in size, management protocols, goals, and profits. Potential breeders are well advised to choose a mentor among those who manage the kind of farm they themselves wish to own and operate. A good mentor will give sound advice and impart much valuable knowledge.

Additionally, the novice livestock breeder must show self-initiative to learn as much as possible. Attendance at seminars, reading books and articles, and exchanging ideas with other farmers should continue throughout a breeder's lifetime. The thirst for knowledge must never stop. The ongoing study of farm infrastructure, soil and pasture management, nutrition, health care, breeding management, birthing protocols, cria care, parasite prevention and treatments, conformation, fiber properties, shearing, and genetics is advisable for the serious breeder.

Breeding decisions need to be made. What will be the farm's specific breeding goals? What will be the criteria for the selection of breeding animals? How will the criteria be supported? If scientific support such as fiber histograms will be utilized, when is the best time to harvest a fiber sample and submit it to the laboratory? Will alpacas that are rejected for breeding by the home farm be sold to others? These questions represent only a tiny sample of options awaiting decisions.

For people with no business background, it is easy to confuse income with profits. A glamorous industry profile, costly marketing campaigns, and the initial purchase of high-priced breeding stock does not necessarily translate into a profitable farm.

Alpacas and their products do not sell themselves. Marketing is essential. It need not be expensive. Nevertheless, plans to advertise breeding stock as well as fiber must be formulated and put into place. Where and how will the harvested fiber be processed prior to being sold? Is there a market for raw fleeces? Sales and purchase contracts for breeding stock call for gathering of legal information and advice.

Like any other farming venture, breeding and selling alpacas and their fiber is unlikely to make a person wealthy. Of course, there is money to be made by those who work hard and have an entrepreneurial spirit. How much? Breeders should not expect to support themselves and a family on farm income alone. Very few farmers do so successfully. For a farmer with a small herd and a modest budget, breeding alpacas must be a passion. The lazy, the dabblers, and the dreamers will not succeed and will come to resent the work involved.

People who wish to own alpacas for profit but don't want the work of breeding them should consider ownership of a fiber herd. I would only advise fiber artists to begin such a program if there is plenty of grazing available to the animals. I personally can't imagine making a profit with a fiber herd kept on dirt lots and fed only expensive hay and processed grain supplements. Others may disagree. Potential fiber herd owners—with or without pastures—should do some very careful financial calculations before committing serious money to such an investment.

In my opinion, alpacas are not suitable for petting zoos, and I have refused selling to petting zoo owners on numerous occasions. Most alpacas don't like to be petted. I've discussed the issue of maladjusted alpacas in a previous chapter. The warnings bear repeating. Beware of super-friendly alpaca "puppy dogs." Males that are given lots of human attention as youngsters will often become aggressive toward humans when they reach sexual maturity. Many females will also become difficult to work with once they've been over-handled as crias. This problem is growing because too many irresponsible breeders either don't care or are purposely not educating buyers.

On the bright side, there is a definite place for alpacas in agricultural tourism. Alpacas can successfully attract customers to a business not directly related to livestock. For example, owners of bed and breakfast establishments or plant nurseries selling retail may wish to maintain alpacas for the enjoyment of their guests or customers. A pasture can be designed to allow guests a full view of the animals but without the opportunity to touch them.

"Won't visitors be disappointed?" a prospective alpaca owner asked me once.

Of course they'll be disappointed. Some may even become angry and won't return. The business owner should remember, though, that while customers may be ignorant of alpaca behavior in the truest sense of the word, most are not stupid. While a few will not return, others will take their place when word spreads about a business that stresses animal welfare. Not only will customers understand a thoughtful explanation of why prey animals are fearful of strangers, they will appreciate the business owner's interest in his or her alpacas' well-being.

People living in cities and suburbs are increasingly concerned about how farmers treat their livestock. Customers have been known to flock to a farm or business with good animal care protocols. Of course, they'll want to touch alpaca fiber, but it doesn't have to be on a live animal. Alpaca fiber samples, skeins of yarn, and felted pieces can all attractively be displayed for customers and guests to touch, stroke, squeeze and, hopefully, purchase.

The Stormwind Farm booth offers a variety of alpaca products to customers.

Animal lovers with small acreage may wish to own alpacas without a profit motive. A few alpacas will not be expensive to maintain. Cost per animal is comparable to that for keeping a sheep or goat. Properly housed, fed, and gently handled, non-breeding alpacas should rarely need veterinary attention, but daily care requires a little more than just throwing hay over the fence.

For some budgets, keeping even the minimum of two alpacas may be too costly. In 1998, my first potential customers were a young couple. Their property was perfect for a small herd of alpacas. As we walked the pasture, they expressed concern over the cost of a water bucket with a heater element. At that point, I strongly advised them not to buy alpacas until their finances were ready to keep up with their desires.

I know more than a few dog owners who plunged into debt over pet expenses. When money is so tight that a child's visit to the dentist must be sacrificed for a pet's feed bill, it's time to re-evaluate family priorities. Likewise, I've witnessed financial tragedies among alpaca breeders. Most could have been prevented with a little common sense and hard work.

When I first planned this book, this chapter's title was *Alpacas as Livestock and Pets*. After writing myself into an emotional lather over the concept of a petting zoo, I thought, no, this isn't right. The word *"pets"* implies that alpacas enjoy being petted, and maybe even that they should be petted. Since they don't, is it right then to advertise and promote their use as pets? If two or three alpacas kept for the sheer enjoyment of their company shouldn't be called pets, what should they be called?

It wasn't a stretch to have the term *company* lead to the word *companion*. Consulting the dictionary, I found this definition: *a person employed to live or travel with another*. Alpacas are not people, but they are companions to one another as defined in my *Webster's New World Dictionary*. They live with other alpacas. Their travels with others may take them to the next state, across country, or simply from one end of the pasture to the other.

The description can be extended to include their human caretakers. If living "with another" means being physically present and spending time with another living creature, my alpacas certainly qualify as my companions. Pasture companions, to be sure, but companions nevertheless. Once I was satisfied with this new designation, I changed the title of the book's chapter in my first, handwritten draft.

My usual *modus operandi* is to write an article or chapter in longhand. The first draft is put aside for at least several weeks, sometimes months. When I review it after a waiting period, I look at my writing with fresh eyes and almost always make numerous changes while writing the second, also handwritten, draft of the manuscript.

The first draft for this book was written in the early summer weeks of 2009. As is my custom, I then stored the manuscript in a handwoven basket and ignored it. The autumn edition of *Alpacas Magazine* brought a surprise. It featured an article written by Marty McGee Bennett titled *Alpacas: Livestock or Pets?* Essentially, Marty made the same points that I do, preferring the term *companion* to *pet*. Of course, Marty's article goes into more detail than this chapter.

I should not have been surprised over our identical terminology. I wrote earlier that, on Stormwind Farm, alpacas are handled, herded, and trained according to Marty's *Camelidynamics* program.

Here's a quote from Marty that, to me, sums up my own philosophy: *"I really love and enjoy alpacas but I love them for what and who they are. I respect their character and do my best to behave in a way that alpacas find to be pleasant and safe. I don't expect them to violate their nature to please me. This approach makes my alpacas more companionable and it also makes them easier to work with and manage."*

The important message here is that *all* alpacas benefit from species-appropriate handling and training. This includes those raised and maintained strictly as livestock.

In the context of my chapter, I initially used the term *pasture companions* to describe alpacas that are kept solely for enjoyment or perhaps educational purposes but without a profit motive.

Marty McGee Bennett's article encouraged me to examine my narrow definition. She points out that alpacas can be both livestock and companion animals, "maybe even at the same time." I think she is right. When we study the history of camelids, we discover that those two concepts were always blurred and overlapped.

In *The Complete Alpaca Book*, Eric Hoffman relates a conversation between Felix, a graduate student in anthropology and Nolberto, a herder in the Andean highlands. One night, the llamas and alpacas are cushed around them, with "their legs folded snugly under their wooly bodies."

According to Hoffman, Felix asks Nolberto, "If all the alpacas and llamas died, what would happen?"

"We would die," Nolberto replied.

"Why?"

"Because we raise alpacas and llamas and they raise us."

After telling readers this charming story, Hoffman, one of North

America's pioneer alpaca breeders, explains how the herders "share a kinship bond with their alpacas and llamas, a bond cemented by tradition, religious devotion, genuine affection, and harsh pragmatism."

The alpacas of Stormwind Farm fit the model of serving as both breeding stock as well as pasture companions.

In the early years, the focus of the North American alpaca industry was primarily centered on breeding animals for profit. There will always be farmers and breeders. There will also always be people who simply enjoy owning livestock without any profit motive. Their animals are pasture companions in the purest sense of the word. We can safely assume that these owners have fun with their alpacas. With the alpaca population expanding, there are thousands of alpacas that would make perfect, not-for-profit pasture companions. They would not be expected to earn their keep. Many owners of small, rural properties would welcome these quiet, undemanding creatures if they realized how much enjoyment can be gained by their presence. Caring for two to four alpaca pasture companions does not require much effort. Freed from many of the chores livestock breeders must attend to, owners of not-for-profit pasture companions simply spend time with their animals.

A good example of someone who enjoys her camelid pasture companions is my friend, Judy. A few years ago, Judy purchased two llamas with plans to possibly start a breeding program. She was also interested in cart driving and using the llamas as therapy animals. Unfortunately, Judy did not purchase Chocolate and Oreo from a reputable breeder. She received no meaningful mentoring. The little advice she was given was counterproductive to establishing a good relationship with the animals. When we met, Judy had no means to herd and catch her llamas. There was a cozy, sturdy barn but no catch pen or well-fitting halters. Oreo and Chocolate fought periodically, as is normal for intact males. Since their fighting teeth had never been filed, Oreo inflicted considerable damage to Chocolate's ear which needed to be stitched and treated.

Other than the minor surgery performed on Chocolate's ear, the llamas had not been touched in several years. Judy felt bad about this and was willing to do anything to rectify the situation.

I contacted Dr. Pettit who was more than willing to help. He administered a mild tranquilizer to the llamas. While Dr. Pettit filed their fighting teeth, injected a de-wormer, and checked their overall condition, Judy and I tackled the shearing. The hand shears I had brought with me removed the llamas' fleeces in large sheets of felted mats. Underneath the mats, the llamas' condition was excellent, a tribute to Judy's good nutritional program and other loving care.

Prior to these long overdue procedures, Judy had purchased livestock panels, a herding tape, and well fitting halters. She was utterly amazed when I showed her how easy it was to herd and confine the llamas minutes before Dr. Pettit's arrival.

A few months later, Dr. Pettit's daughter, veterinarian Dr. Jeannette Pettit, gelded both llamas and took care of inoculations. Chocolate and Oreo were anesthetized prior to the surgery. Dr. Pettit had Judy bring hay bales to the surgery site to prop up their necks and heads. This prevented regurgitation and possible fatal choking while the llamas were under anesthesia. Again, Judy was surprised and delighted over how little time and effort it took to catch her pasture companions prior to their surgical procedures.

After Oreo and Chocolate had recovered and returned to their spacious pasture, Judy and I relaxed with cups of freshly brewed coffee. With both of us resting comfortably on the hay bales, Judy told me about her childhood. She grew up in a Pennsylvania Mennonite community.

"My friends can't understand why I love to garden and enjoy the llamas so much," Judy said, "but I was raised among animals and gardens."

Judy and her husband live in a beautifully maintained and decorated historic home. A carefully planned, modern addition adds to the charm of the old house. From the addition, a brick patio and walkway lead past flower gardens and a lawn area all the way to the small barn and the spacious pasture beyond. Woods surround and shelter the property. Judy and her husband tend to several bee hives placed on the lawn. A variety of vegetables and flowers grow adjacent to the attractive fence next to the llamas' barn.

From the patio, the gardens and pasture appear like a paradise, with the two llamas grazing like magical unicorns in the distance. Oreo and Chocolate share their barn and pasture with a tiny rooster and an even tinier hen. The llamas are very protective of their little flock. When I was there, they chased Judy's dog when it snuck into the pasture and ran after the chickens.

While talking to Judy, I once again noticed the generous dimensions of Oreo's and Chocolate's pasture with great delight and approval. All too often, pasture companions are confined in pens or enclosures that severely restrict their movement. Many of these unlucky creatures wallow in mud during rainy weather and don't find a blade of grass during the grazing seasons. Judy's llamas are lucky!

"I quickly lost interest in breeding llamas," Judy told me that day, "but I've never regretted having Oreo and Chocolate share my life." She feels pleasure when she sees her llamas as she tends to her gardens and small bee colony. "Since I've discovered that Oreo and Chocolate love pieces of apple and grapes, I bring them treats every day," Judy beamed.

For prey animals that have hardly been touched, let alone handled and trained, the llamas were amazingly calm when we had to herd, catch, and halter them. Of course, like Marty, Judy treats her pasture companions with respect and accepts them on their terms.

Unlike Judy, many people who profess to love animals expect them to perform functions and fulfill human needs that are not in their nature. For example, there's my friend, Annie, who loves her cat dearly but would prefer her to act like a dog. My husband, David, cannot tolerate the fact that our Whippets chase and kill rabbits and other small animals that venture into the fenced dog yard. He would like them to live in peace with the wildlife intruders. People buy alpacas and llamas and describe them as "stupid" when the camelids react with fear and panic to novel stimuli. They would like to see them display the trust and obedience of a fellow submissive predator. Those are all unrealistic expectations. Animals have no choice but to accept us the way we are even though I readily admit that dogs are geniuses in manipulating their owners. Why can't humans accept and appreciate the unique traits of other species?

Alpacas are a wonderful choice as pasture companions if we enjoy and respect the characteristics that define them as alpacas. What humans perceive as limitations are merely alpacas behaving like alpacas.

"So are you saying," a visitor once asked me, "that alpacas should never be touched?"

Not at all. With proper handling and training, all alpacas can be taught to calmly accept human touches.

Alpacas are successfully used in 4-H projects. To see small children navigate complex obstacle courses with their alpacas is a special treat. Children are some of the best handlers of alpacas I've ever seen. I think that many are more skilled than adults because they don't have preconceived ideas about what an alpaca should be and how it must perform. They don't hold their breaths in agitated suspense while they work with their animals.

In her terrific book *Animals in Translation*, Dr. Temple Grandin writes:

"People and animals are supposed to be together. We spent quite a long time evolving together, and we used to be partners. Now people are cut off from animals unless they have a dog or a cat."

Although the focus of this particular passage in Dr. Grandin's book was on the ownership of horses, her words apply to many other species as well. Alpaca pasture companions could certainly also be described as pasture partners in a healthy outdoor lifestyle. People who own alpacas often engage in wholesome activities that are enjoyed by the whole family.

Livestock, pasture companions, pasture pals, pasture partners—does it really matter which label we assign to our alpacas? What truly matters is that we treat them with the respect all creatures deserve, especially those that live in our service.

In several of my previous writings, I quoted a poem written by Ella Wheeler-Wilcox. I will include it here as well. It's a fitting ending to this chapter. After that, nothing more needs to be said.

> I am the voice of the voiceless;
> Through me the dumb shall speak,
> Till the deaf world's ear be made to hear
> The wrongs of the worldless weak.
> And I am my brother's keeper
> And I will fight his fight;
> And speak the word for beast and bird
> Till the world shall set things right.

Ella Wheeler-Wilcox (1850-1919)

Afterword

Any time an author writes about animals, there's the issue of pronouns. Is an animal an *it* or a *he/she*? My *Webster's New World Dictionary* gives, among others, this definition for *it*: *the animal or thing previously mentioned or under discussion.* When I looked up *he*, I read this explanation: *the man, boy or male animal previously mentioned.*

The author of a book on English grammar insists that the correct pronoun for an animal should always be *it*, with *he* and *she* reserved for human beings. Another author, writing about welfare issues of pets and livestock, makes the point that applying the pronoun *it* to a live creature is disrespectful. Friends whom I polled on the subject expressed various views and opinions. Furthermore, applying the pronoun *it* obviously did not work whenever I referred to my alpacas and dogs by their call names in the same or a previous sentence.

For a while, I dithered back and forth. Finally, I arrived at a compromise. Readers may have noticed a pattern in my application of pronouns. Whenever I wrote about an alpaca, a dog, or other non-human creature in general terms or simply as a member of its species, I used the pronoun *it* to refer to a previously mentioned individual. For example, the escaped monkey that visited our farm was an *it*, as in: It frolicked in our backyard. I changed to *he/she* in the case of an alpaca or dog known to me by a personal call name.

I hope this solution satisfied those readers who pay strict attention to the correct usage of our language. Of course, I sincerely hope that my choice did not detract from the pleasure of reading the book.

Some readers may be interested in updated information on the alpaca population of Stormwind Farm. Our website (www.StormwindAlpacas. com) provides this information as well as a selection of educational articles about raising alpacas.

To all who purchased and read *The Alpacas of Stormwind Farm*: Thank you very much!

About the Author

Ingrid Wood was born and raised in Germany. Her life-long fascination with farming and breeding livestock traces back to wonderful childhood vacations spent with relatives on their farms. One of her grandfathers was a bee keeper. An uncle tended the family's vineyards; a great-aunt kept dairy cows. Others raised pigs, chickens, and small flocks of sheep. All were inspiring role models for a young girl with an interest in raising livestock and living on a farm.

In 1970, Ingrid followed her American-born husband, David, to the United States of America. After raising their son, Benjamin, in the historical town of Mount Holly, New Jersey, the Woods moved a few miles from their suburban home to a small farm they purchased in Springfield Township. The first alpacas arrived on Stormwind Farm in 1997.

In addition to raising alpacas, Ingrid's interests include writing, reading non-fiction books, gardening, spinning the fine fiber of her camelids, and playing with her grandchildren. Considerable time is devoted to caring for the Stormwind Whippets. On weekends, Ingrid enjoys selling fleeces and other alpacas products at agricultural fairs and festivals. She also sponsors numerous, annual educational events on Stormwind Farm (for more information, visit www.StormwindAlpacas.com).

Ingrid's articles have been published in *The* LAMA LETTER, *The GALA Newsletter, American Livestock Magazine,* MAPACA *Newsletter, Alpacas Magazine, The International Camelid Quarterly* and the German camelid publication LAMAS. Her first book, *A Breeder's Guide to Genetics – Relax, it's not Rocket Science,* was published in 2004.

Made in the USA
San Bernardino, CA
12 December 2013